Introduction

Y Bala – meaning 'the outflow of the lake'– has a beautiful setting on the shores of Llyn Tegid, the largest natural lake in Wales, surrounded by hills and mountains. It lies within the southern area of the Snowdonia National Park on a natural fault that has provided an important route into the heartland of Wales since prehistoric times, and later became part of the Roman road system. At the heart of the district of Penllyn, the town was created in 1310 by Roger de Mortimer to reinforce English control of the district.

Despite its English origins, Y Bala is a strong Welsh-speaking community that has produced renowned poets, politicians and preachers, who have helped to shape cultural and religious life in Wales, and further afield in Patagonia. In the 18th and early 19thC the town was renowned for its knitted woollen gloves, stockings and caps. Today, it retains its status as a small market town for the local farming community, and as a centre of the Welsh language and culture.

The area is well known for its watersports, but it is also excellent walking country. This new fully revised third edition of my guidebook explores its diverse scenery and history through 22 walks. It includes a few new walks, routes to hilltop forts and viewpoints accessible on Open Access land, as well as two linear walks (21 & 22) between Y Bala and Llanuwchllyn, now sections of Snowdonia National Park's superb waymarked upland circular trail around Llyn Tegid.

There are walks across pastureland, over open hills and moorland, by rivers and lakes, through woods and forests. They offer extensive views and visit many places of historical interest. The routes, which range from 1½ – 9 miles, follow public rights of way or permissive paths. A key feature is that most routes, as well as containing shorter walk options, can easily be linked to provide longer and more challenging day walks, if required.

Ensure that you are suitably equipped, especially on the more exposed higher routes. Walking boots are recommended, along with appropriate clothing to protect against the elements. Please remember that the condition of paths can vary according to season and weather, forest growth and clearance. If you encounter any problems with Rights of Way, please refer these to Gwynedd Council (www.gwynedd.gov.uk).

Each walk has a detailed map and description, but be aware that changes in detail can occur at any time. The location of each walk is shown on the back cover and a summary of their key features is also given. This includes an estimated walking time, but allow more time to enjoy the scenery. Please observe the country co

Enjoy your walking!

WALK I
Y BALA

DESCRIPTION A 4 mile orientation walk around Y Bala – a good introduction to the town, its history, notable buildings, and its scenic setting alongside Llyn Tegid, the rivers Tryweryn and Dee, surrounded by hills and mountains. Allow at least 3 hours for there is much to see. The route can easily be undertaken as two separate walks of 2½ and 1½ miles, and offers different starting points.

START Pont-y-Bala [SH 929362]

DIRECTIONS The stone bridge of Pont-y-Bala, which carries the A494 over the Afon Tryweryn, lies near the fire-station at the eastern edge of town. A car park and toilets are nearby.

I Walk across Pont y Bala to see the old stone arched gateway to Rhiwlas. Return across the bridge then cross the road to go through a small gate opposite. Follow the signposted Tegid Way along a wide grass flood embankment near the Afon Tryweryn, then past the gated entrance to Bala sluice house and along another embanked path near the river. Shortly the path angles away to briefly join the infant river Dee – *which enters the lake at Llanuwchllyn as the Afon Dyfrdwy and is said to pass through 'without mingling the standing waters'* – before reaching the B4391. Cross to the pavement opposite. Turn RIGHT and continue with the Tegid Way along the nearby side road past the end of Llyn Tegid – *enjoying great views along the lake.*

2 At a car park, continue with the Tegid Way along a surfaced path near the shoreline of the lake. *Llyn Tegid, 4 miles long, nearly ¾ miles wide, and up to over 140 feet deep, is the largest freshwater lake in Wales. It contains the unique gwyniad – a whitefish member of the herring family imprisoned here after the Ice Age, when the lake was formed. The lake is rich in legends. One says that the lake is named after the mythical prince, Tegid Foel, whose town was one night engulfed by the huge lake in vengeance for his cruelty to his subjects. Another is that*

the valley was flooded after the keeper of St Gywair's holy well, forgot to replace the lid. Eventually, you pass behind the Leisure Centre, then above a lakeside car park to reach the A494 by Loch Café. Turn RIGHT along the road towards the town centre. Just past the cinema, take the road on the left by the garage.

3 On the bend, take an enclosed path rising along a field edge to a road. Go up the road to the entrance to Bala golf club, after which the road begins to descend. Shortly take the signposted path into Hendre Ddu's access track on the right. Cross a stile by the gate and go along the field edge passing above the house, and on to a stile/gate in the corner. Go along the next field edge, over another stile, and on to a stone ruin ahead. Here the waymarked path turns LEFT past an old stone gatepost and continue along the top field edge across Craig y Fron, soon passing the remains of impressive caverns with stone pillar supports. *Stone was quarried here for the construction of Capel Tegid and other prominent buildings in Y Bala.* At their end the path bends down to a stile and continues down the field edge to another stile. Follow the enclosed path past dwellings to a road. Follow it RIGHT across the junction and down past the football ground and school into town. At cross-roads, follow the road RIGHT back to the garage passed earlier. Cross the main road.

4 Continue along the High Street past an old stone building – *the former Aran Factory shop, originally a workhouse in the mid-19thC* – then the 17thC Ye Old Bull's Head and Barclay's Bank – *the former home of Thomas Charles (1755-1814), the great revivalist preacher. He came to the town in 1784, becoming one of the leaders of Welsh Methodism. He established the Sunday School system in Wales, wrote and published childrens' religious books, and produced cheap bibles which promoted literacy in North Wales. He also helped to found the British and Foreign Bible Society in 1804 after being inspired by Mary Jones. In 1860, 16 year old Mary, a poor weaver's daughter from Llanfihangel-y-Pennant, a hamlet lying*

behind the Cadair Idris range, walked bare-foot 25 miles over the mountains to Y Bala to buy a bible from him. Unfortunately he had sold them all, but he was so impressed with her efforts that he gave her his own copy.

5 Turn RIGHT down Tegid Street, past a traditional ironmongers shop and on to reach Capel Tegid. *The chapel, built in 1866 in memory of Thomas Charles, whose statue is nearby, was an important landmark of Nonconformist Wales.* Return to the High Street, then cross over to the 18thC White Lion Royal Hotel. *George Borrow, author of 'Wild Wales', stayed here twice during his walking tour in 1854. His lavish breakfast included eggs, mutton chops, salmon, trout and potted shrimps. He wrote 'I had never previously seen such a breakfast set before me'. The word 'Royal' was later added after Queen Victoria called at the hotel during her visit to Y Bala in 1889.* Continue along the High Street – *opposite is the former 19thC Town Hall* – to reach the statue of Thomas Edward Ellis (1859-99) – *a Liberal MP and*

Chief Whip, who strove to achieve Welsh home rule, the disestablishment of the church in Wales, and better education. Go along Berwyn Street opposite. At its end on the left is the former Independent College (1842-86) – *where Michael D Jones succeeded his father as Principal. He was a promoter of the venture in 1865, when 153 men, women and children sailed from Liverpool to establish a Welsh community in Patagonia, South America. Their descendants maintain strong ties with Wales, and many still speak Welsh.*

6 Turn LEFT to reach the gated entrance to Tomen y Bala – *believed to be a late 11thC Norman castle mound. It was later used for open-air preaching and by woollen knitters.* Continue to the junction, then turn RIGHT to finish at Neuadd y Cyfnod. *Originally a 17thC house, it was converted by Edmund Meyrick to a Free School in 1713. In the mid-19thC, it was rebuilt, with the main hall a replica of the one in Jesus College, Oxford, and it became a grammar school.*

WALK 2

PEN Y BWLCH GWYN & MOEL EMOEL

DESCRIPTION A 9 mile figure of eight walk (**A**, through the varied countryside north of Y Bala, with extensive views. The main route rises in stages to explore a wild remote area of Open Access land, crossing Pen y Bwlch Gwyn (1646ft/502 metres). It then either skirts (route B) or climbs (route A) the prominent hill of Moel Emoel (1801ft/549metres) for superb views, passes an attractive upland lake, before crossing undulating country to finish with delightful riverside walking. Allow about 5½ hours. This is for experienced hillwalkers only and should be avoided in poor visibility. An easier 3 mile walk (**B**) is included which avoids the open hill section.

START Near Pont Ty'n-y-ddol on the A4212 [SH 913384].

DIRECTIONS From Y Bala take the A4212 road towards Trawsfynydd. After about 1½ miles, it crosses the river (Pont Ty'n-y-ddol). 200 yards further is a small parking area on the right. Please do not block gateways. Alternatively, use a lay-by just before the river bridge.

I Cross the stile at the gated entrance to Berth. Follow the road, then access track up to the farm, bending LEFT past outbuildings. Go through a waymarked gate on the right. Go half-LEFT up the field, through a boundary gap and up the next field edge to cross a stile midway. Continue up past a ruin to a road. Follow it LEFT, then take a signposted path up a track on the right through the edge of a wood. Continue up the field edge to a stile in the top corner. Keep ahead up the slope, over a track, and on up to a gate in a fence corner by Penmaen-mawr. (For **Walk B** turn right and resume text at point 5)

2 Go through the gate and follow the fence on your left past a waymarked gate and on up along the edge of an old reedy sunken track. Cross a stile in the fence and another one ahead. Go up the right-hand side of a tree

boundary/ sunken track to cross a stile at its end. Follow the walled path up to a forestry track. Go along the green track opposite to a gate. Go past a barn, then a small plantation, and on to a gate at another plantation corner – *with a view west of Llyn Celyn.*Follow the green track ahead across upland pasture – *with a view east to Moel Emoel and Llyn Maen Bras* – to a gate. When it splits take its right fork, shortly bending up and continuing below a fence to a gate into Open Access land. Descend to another gate by mature trees, go past the nearby ruin, and on down to a gate. Follow the path ahead above an old embanked stone boundary to another gate. Keep ahead, soon on a rising path beneath the fence to a stile. Continue up beside the fence to bend RIGHT along a green track to a stile/gate. Follow the narrow green track along the edge of a wide treeless valley up to another gate.

3 Continue along the track, soon bending right then left and rising, then crossing the wide top of Pen y Bwlch Gwyn – *enjoying extensive all-round views.* When the fading track angles left continue across the tussocky ground to a fence 100 yards ahead. Follow it RIGHT down to a gate in it. Turn RIGHT along a path to another gate and on towards Moel Emoel, shortly reaching a prominent viewpoint looking towards Llyn Tegid. It then bends right across small rock outcrops and soon splits. Follow the fainter rough left fork across tussocky/reedy ground towards Moel Emoel. After about 50 yards you have a choice. For **route A**, head up to a large boulder, then continue up the northern slopes of Moel Emoel via a ladder-stile to its summit cairn. Follow a good path down its southern slopes. At a cross-path about 200 yards before the forest, turn RIGHT and follow a green track down the hillside to a stile/gate at point 4. For **route B** continue with the improving wide path across the lower western slopes towards Llyn Maen Bras. Later cross a ladder-stile by a gate in the fence descending from Moel Emoel. Angle LEFT to cross a stream about 12 yards from the fence, then continue on an intermittent path across the tusssocky/reedy terrain ahead. Shortly you join the old wide path, which then bends towards Llyn Maen Bras to a stile/gate.

4 Go down the green track to a gate. Cross the track, and descend to a gate ahead. Follow the path down into trees to a stile in a boundary. Continue through the small wood then down the edge of two fields. At the bottom turn RIGHT through a gate in the corner and head half-RIGHT across the part reedy field to the end of a tree boundary. Turn LEFT towards distant pylons to pass between a telegraph pole and a forest, over a stream and past a waymark post. At another stream, turn RIGHT through the tree boundary, cross the stream and follow the path up to a stile. Follow the field edge round to a stile in the corner. Descend, then turn LEFT beside the stream to cross a stile and the stream. Go up a track, then bear RIGHT past a barn and on between a ruin and Penmaen-canol cottage, then turn LEFT through a gate. Go across the field, to a gate across a track. (A near-by field gate ahead gives access to an alternative link route as shown). Go up the track to a stile ahead and follow a path through a small wood. Continue across rough upland pasture guided by posts to eventually pass behind Penmaen-mawr to a familiar gate.

5 Go along its access track. On the bend by a yellow-topped post go along the short green track and up the slope ahead. Continue across the middle of a large field to a stile beyond a tree. Go down the next field to Llwyn Ci farm, then follow its access track to a road. Follow it LEFT for ¼ mile then take a signposted path on the right. Go half-LEFT down the large field towards a farm to a gate in the boundary. Follow a gated green track, then the farm's driveway to a road. Turn RIGHT up the road, then shortly LEFT on a signposted path and follow the gated track down to the Afon Tryweryn. Continue through the large field, then follow a delightful waymarked stiled riverside path through a wood and fields, and continue to the road near the start.

Pen y Bwlch Gwyn

WALK A

Moel Emoel

route B

route A

Llyn Maen Bras

N

0   ¼
mile

Penmaen-Canol

Pylon

Pylons

Penmaen-mawr

① Berth

WALK B

Afon Tryweryn

walk 3

WALK 3
BEYOND LLANFOR

DESCRIPTION A 5½ mile walk (**A**) to the ancient village of Llanfor and through nearby undulating countryside, part of the Rhiwlas estate. Allow about 3¼ hours. The route can easily be shortened to a 4½ mile walk (**B**) from Llanfor or a simple 1½ mile walk (**C**) between Y Bala and Llanfor.

START Pont-y-Bala [SH 929362] or alternatively Llanfor [SH 938367].

DIRECTIONS Pont-y-Bala, which carries the A494 over the Afon Tryweryn, lies at the eastern edge of Y Bala town. A car park and toilets are nearby. Llanfor lies just off the A494 to the east.

L lanfor, now a peaceful village, whose current buildings date back to the 18thC, was once an important settlement.before the creation of Y Bala in the 14thC. The Romans built a fort and marching camp here and in medieval times it was a thriving farming community with regular markets and fairs.

I From the north side of the bridge walk alongside the A494 – *passing the old arched gateway leading to Rhiwlas Hall.* Follow the part-screened pavement past a stile opposite a house and on to cross another stile further along. Go half-RIGHT across the large field to the road at Llanfor. (For **Walk C** turn left up the road to point 5.) Turn RIGHT through the village to the bend near the former church. *Built in 1875, it stands on the site of the oldest church in Meirionydd that once served this large parish. Among the intricately carved headstones is the grave of a man who survived 27 battles, including Waterloo. The unusual large stone building at the top of the churchyard has a tale to tell. The inscription above the doorway reads: 'As to my latter end I go to seek my Jubilee, I bless the good horse Bendigo, who built this tomb for me'. This mausoleum of Richard John Lloyd Price of Rhiwlas Hall – a famous sportsman, author and founder of a short-lived Welsh Whiskey Distillery at Fron Goch – was paid for by a wager on the horse Bendigo that won the Kempton Park Jubilee in the year he died – 1887.*

2 From the bend follow the signposted Tegid Way along a track passing behind the mausoleum in the churchyard to a small metal gate into a field. Angle up the field to join a farm track. *In an adjoining field is the remains of an earthwork castle of late 11thC Norman origin or late Welsh revival.* Go up the track and just past a shale rock-face, as it bends half-right, keep ahead for a few yards. At the fence corner, go across the field towards a transmitter mast on the wooded hillside ahead to pass through an old embanked field boundary by a telegraph pole. At a stream ahead turn RIGHT and follow the bank above it. After passing a solitary tree, leave the stream and continue across reedy ground to go through a way-marked gate in the fence corner ahead. Bear RIGHT then cross the stream. Now follow the path ahead up between trees then across the bracken-covered slope and along the perimeter fence of a wood to cross a stile. Follow the fence up the slope, then up the field edge – *with good views across the Dee valley.*

3 Just before a stile in the top field corner, turn RIGHT alongside the boundary to cross another stile in the fence. Bear RIGHT up to join the fence/tree boundary and follow a stiled path along the edge of two fields, then pass through an old farm. Follow its access track to ford a stream and on to reach a minor road. Follow it LEFT, then shortly turn RIGHT along a forestry road signposted to Creigiau-isaf. When it splits continue along the right fork through the open forest. Shortly it bends left and rises gradually above an area of cleared forest. After crossing a stream and just before the bend of the track, you meet a waymarked path angling back on the right to the nearby secluded cottage of Creigiau-uchaf. Here take a short path on the left between a line of trees and telegraph poles to a stile into a large field. Go towards buildings ahead, later joining a short old sunken green track to the reach the old farm. Turn LEFT past the right-hand side of the stone outbuilding and over a stream. At the hinged side of a wooden gate just beyond turn LEFT and follow the boundary on your right down the field and through the facing gate in the corner – *with views* *of the Berwyns, Llyn Tegid and the Arans.* Turn RIGHT past the telegraph pole up the field edge, then bend LEFT down the edge of woodland to a stile in the field corner. Cross a track and follow a path ahead through birch. After 10 yards turn RIGHT over an embankment and on to cross a nearby stile.

4 Continue between the old embanked tree boundary on your right and woodland, past a waymarked tree stump to pass through stones in the old boundary ahead. At a stony track beyond follow it LEFT over a stream/reedy area. As the track begins to rise before it bends join a path leading RIGHT below a small bracken-covered slope and on across open ground. Pass through a gap just *to walk* to the left of a tele-*walk* graph pole below a *2* pylon – *with a good view of Y Bala and Llyn Tegid.* Just beyond follow the old boundary on your left down to a nearby ruined farm. Continue along its access track, shortly passing a plantation. After a gate at its corner, leave the track and go down the middle of the field to a gate in the corner, and on along the edge of the next reedy field to a stile/gate onto a minor road. Go down the road, over a river, and on to a junction with another road at woodland. Continue down the road, past

a house, an alternative link path, then an Electric substation. As the road descends towards Llanfor, take the signposted Tegid Way through a gate on the right.

5 Follow the path through a delightful narrow area of attractive mature trees, known locally as the 'Lovers Walk', At a boundary corner turn LEFT through a gate, then follow the path down and along the edge of two fields to reach the A494 and your outward route.

7

WALK 4

LLYN CAER-EUNI

DESCRIPTION A 5⅓ mile walk (**A**), with good views, through a little known area of attractive low upland pasture and valleys, passing near an ancient standing stone, and the site of a cock pit, to visit a delightful hidden lake, lying at 1040 ft/317 metres. Allow about 3 hours. The route can easily be shortened to a 4 mile walk (**B**).

START Sarnau [SH 972393].

DIRECTIONS Leave Y Bala on the A494 towards Corwen, and after about 4 miles, turn left into the hamlet of Sarnau. Park tidily on the roadside.

Sarnau *was once an important crossing point of two ancient routes. Before a turnpike road.(now the A494) was built the main valley road went through the village. It had an inn and a smithy. The first stone house on the left (note the arch in the gable end) has an interesting history. It was built as a church, but before it was consecrated, it was used as a hospital after smallpox broke out in the area. It later became a church school. Opposite Sarnau is Coers y Sarnau nature reserve, a patchwork of wetland habitat and woodland owned by the North Wales Wildlife Trust.*

Continue up the road, then take the side road on the left between houses. Go up the road, then take a signposted path along a track on the left – *with good views west to the Arans.* Follow it up to Ty Hen. Just before the house, cross a stile on the left by a small stone building. Turn RIGHT along the field edge to a track. Turn RIGHT a few yards then LEFT up the field edge round to cross a stile near a gate. Turn RIGHT to enter another field and go along its edge. In the corner follow the fence RIGHT passing behind a cottage and round to a small gate in it onto the cottage's access track. Follow it to a road. *Prominent among the reedy pasture is a standing stone, which once marked the line of an old road from Llangwm to Llandderfel.*

Ahead at the road is Coed y Bedo, a small old Welsh Manor house, once the home of Bedo Aeddren, a 15thC poet. Turn LEFT (or right for **Walk B**) and follow the road down the valley, then take the first side road on the right. Follow the tree-lined road up the attractive wooded side valley. After a gate, the road enters a more open section of the valley.

2 Just after a waymarked path on the left, go through a waymarked gate on the right. Go up the field to a small gate in the top left-hand corner onto a green track. Go slightly right up the slope ahead, passing between clumps of trees, then continue across upland pasture above a small wooded side valley to a ladder-stile ahead. Keep ahead across rougher terrain, then angle LEFT up to a stone stile. Follow an old green track down and along a small bracken and reed covered valley to a gate into Open Access land. Here you can simply follow the track to its bend and nearby stile. A more rewarding alternative is to turn RIGHT across tussocky ground to pass the first pylon, climb onto the nearby ridge top for extensive all-round views, then head NE over subsidiary tops to descend to the bend of the track. *Alongside the track is a small circular mound – the remains of a cock pit. Cockfighting was once popular in the area.* Cross the stile ahead and follow the boundary on the left down to a road. Follow it LEFT, soon descending into the attractive wooded valley of Cwm Main – *once occupied by Quakers.*

3 On the bend at the bottom of the hill, turn RIGHT on the signposted path up the access lane to Rhydywernen and Maes Tegfryn, then take its right fork past the end of early 19thC Capel Rhydywernen – *still serving the local community.* Descend between the cottage and an outbuilding to a gate and on down an old enclosed green track to another gate and a footbridge over a stream beyond. Turn LEFT and follow the stream along the edge of a long field to a stile. Follow the path past conifers and on to another stile. Continue along the bottom edge of an area of young trees, past a footbridge over an adjoining stream to a stile. Go along

Cwm Main

③

Chapel

Llyn Caer-Euni

④

walk ▷ 5

link path

Cock pit

②

Coed y bedo

standing °stone

walk 5

link path

N

0 ¼ mile

Ty Hen

① Sarnau

A494 to Corwen

Cors y Sarnau

to Y Bala

the field, then after about 120 yards at the fence corner bear RIGHT up to a waymark post by gorse at the bottom of woodland. Follow an improving path rising across the wooded slope to cross a stile. Turn LEFT, then after 15 yards, angle RIGHT up beside the moss-covered remains of an old wall, part hidden in undergrowth, through the trees for 40 yards onto a hidden stony track. Follow the waymarked path opposite up a green track through trees. At the end of the wood, when the track swings sharp right, go through the gate ahead and across a stream. Follow an old sunken reedy path ahead, soon bending right, then continue to an old stone sheepfold ahead. *Almost unexpectedly, just ahead lie the tranquil waters of Llyn Caer-Euni. It is said that here late at night you may see a horned shepherd collecting his sheep – reputed to be Cernunnos the Celtic God of Nature and the Underworld.*

4 Follow a path angling LEFT to large boulders at the lakeside – *a scenic stopping place.* Continue along the end of the lake, boggy in places. At its corner, go half-RIGHT away from the lake on an intermittent path over wet tussock ground to pass

the left-hand side of a rock covered slope ahead. Continue in the same direction, soon rising across the edge of higher heather-covered ground ahead, then up a reedy slope. Go past a gate in the boundary to your right, to level out at a stile in it beneath a rocky crag – *with good views of the Berwyn Range, the Arans, Cadair Idris, and Arenig Fawr.* Continue westwards across tussocky ground following the wall on your left, soon on a gradually improving green track to join a wide stony track, which becomes a road at a gate. Follow it down to the start – *enjoying good views of Llyn Tegid.*

9

WALK 5
CAER EUNI

DESCRIPTION A meandering 5½ mile walk (**A**), with extensive views, exploring an attractive upland area of Open Access, once occupied by early man. It visits two important early historical sites – an impressive Iron-Age hillfort (1197 feet/365 metres high) and Bronze Age circular cairns. The route includes a shorter 3 mile walk (**B**) and can easily be varied to include Llyn Caer-Euni. Allow about 3½ hours.

START Bethel [SH 988398].

DIRECTIONS Leave Y Bala on the A494 towards Corwen, and after nearly 5 miles, upon reaching the hamlet of Bethel, turn left on a minor road opposite the B4402 (Llandderfel). A small parking space is immediately on the left.

Bethel, so named after a chapel was built here in the early 19thC, was an important stopping place for drovers. They stayed at The Boot – an inn up to the 1930s – and their cattle were kept in a field opposite. There was a smithy, and at one time a school. The minor road is on the line of the Roman road running east from Caergai to Chester.

I Walk along the road past the former chapel, and on past Blaen Cwm. About 150 yards further, before another house, do a sharp U-turn LEFT on a signposted path up a rough track back across the young tree-covered slope, soon bending sharp right and rising steadily past side tracks to a stile. Continue ahead near the boundary, in the field corner bending LEFT to a ladder-stile. Follow the old embanked boundary ahead up to cross another stile. Bear RIGHT to follow a path along slightly higher and drier ground parallel with the nearby fence to join a track. Follow it for about 50 yards, then just before a gate across it, turn LEFT along a path across reedy ground, following the tree/fence boundary on the right to go through a facing gateway in the corner. Follow a path ahead up to cross the ramparts and ditch of Caer Euni hillfort and on to its large summit cairn for all-round views. *The long narrow hillfort, overlooking an important ancient*

route. utilises a steep slope on its south-east side, with ramparts and a ditch on its north-west side, and an entrance at the north-east. It was later enlarged and strengthened to the south-west. The site contains evidence of roundhouses and three Bronze Age burial cairns. Return to the gateway, then bear RIGHT along a path near the fence, after a few yards bending LEFT to follow a choice of paths down to join the fence on your right to cross a stile by a gate in it to join a cross-path beyond. (For **Walk B** follow it left up to the stone circles.)

2 Turn RIGHT down the path and across the field passing to the left of an old stile/fence and continuing to a gate onto a road. Go up the road. At a signposted cross-path, turn LEFT down the access track to Tyn-yr-Erw and cross a stile to the left of the cottage. Turn LEFT along the reedy field edge and through a gate in the corner. Follow the path leading half-RIGHT to a waymark post amongst gorse, then turn RIGHT down through trees, over a stream, and past another waymark post to a ladder-stile. Go down the field to a stile in the right-hand corner and down the next field edge to cross another stile. Turn LEFT and cross a nearby moss covered wall. Now follow a path, guided by a series of waymark posts down through the wood to a stony track at its corner near a short gated walled section. (If you emerge from the wood lower down follow the track left.)

3 Go through the gate opposite, then turn LEFT up the field edge, through an old gateway and on down the next field edge – *with the attractive wooded valley of Cwm Main, once occupied by Quakers, ahead* – to cross a stile on the left. Go across tussocky ground and through trees to reach a green track leading from a nearby small corrugated shed. Follow it RIGHT, soon fading, then continue ahead on a waymarked path alongside the fence of a game-bird rearing area to a stile. The path continues along the bottom edge of attractive woodland, shortly rising to a gateway, then across the more open slope to a gate onto an access track. About 15 yards beyond a cattle-grid, as the track descends towards restored Tyddyn Tyfod – *once occupied by Edward ap Rhys, who went with the first group of Welsh Quakers to Pennsylvania in 1682* – turn LEFT on a waymarked path up between the fence and a tree boundary to a stile. Continue up the enclosed path across the hillside.

4 At the top turn LEFT through a gate just before a stile (a link path to Llyn Caer-Euni). Turn LEFT and follow a path along the moorland edge, over a stream at the top of a gully, then towards a solitary large tree ahead. Just before it go up the slope ahead to the highest point for all-round views (or continue past the tree, taking the path's right fork beneath the craggy slopes) then descend south. At the bottom of the slope turn LEFT to a stile in the fence. Keep ahead, then just before a boundary corner, turn RIGHT to the other boundary corner. Continue ahead up and across short tussocky ground to a clear cross path. Follow it RIGHT to the remains of Cefn Caer-Euni bronze age stone circles at a good viewpoint. *The large kerb circle and a smaller ring cairn were used for ceremonial and burial purposes. The large circle was said to have been used as a cockpit in the 18thC when cockfighting was popular in the area.*

5 Continue along the path to a small gate, then head slightly LEFT on a path across the broad moorland ridge towards the Arans to go through the right of two gates. Turn LEFT and immediately before the other gate turn RIGHT along an improving path/ old reedy track – *soon with a view of Llyn Caer-Euni nestling below* – passing close to the small ridge on the left to cross a stile beyond its end. Turn LEFT and follow the old then new fence down to a stile/gate near the wood corner. Follow a path ahead down below the fence, then do a sharp u-turn RIGHT down an old reedy track to a waymarked gateway and old stile. Now go down the left-hand edge of the old part tree-lined sunken track and past the side of a house to the road by the start.

Map labels: Cwm Main, Tyn-yr-Erw, N, Tyddyn Ty fod, 0 ¼ mile, fort, walk 4, Llyn Caer-Euni, circles, walk 4, Blaen Cwm, Bethel, to Y Bala, A494, B4402, to Llanderfel

Llyn Caer-Euni

WALK 6
MYNYDD MYNYLLOD

DESCRIPTION This meandering 7½ mile walk (**A**) rises from the Upper Dee valley through its part wooded lower slopes to explore delightful hidden upland pasture and moorland north east of Llandderfel. It rises in easy stages to just over 1200 feet/370 metres and offers superb views. Allow about 4 hours. It can easily be shortened to 4½ mile walk (**B**), or varied using the link road shown on the map.
START Llandderfel [SH 982371].
DIRECTIONS See Walk 7 for directions and information on Llanderfel.

1 Follow the road over the stream and up to a junction, then keep ahead past a former chapel. *It contained an 1868 commemorative stone to John Jones, Ellis Roberts and Mary Jones (mother of Michael D Jones - the founder of the Patagonia community) who were turned out of their homes after the 1859 Election by their Tory landlords for voting for a Liberal MP. Like others, they had become empowered from learning to read through religion and posed a threat to the landed gentry. The stone is now in the Neuadd Derfel. Follow the road out of the village – soon enjoying good views of the river Dee.*

2 After ¾ mile, take a signposted path through a gate on the left, opposite Dolgadfa. Go up the field to a stile above a stream into a wood. Follow a path ahead along the bottom wood edge, then at a gate in the fence turn LEFT up a wider path. Soon leave it to angle RIGHT up to follow the top boundary fence to a stile. Continue through the trees beneath the fence to its corner. Just beyond bear RIGHT along a path, soon rising to a yellow-topped post. The path continues across the wooded slope past another post, then bends up to a small gate into a field. Continue ahead beside the fence, then turn RIGHT through a gate. Follow the way-marked permissive path ahead down to a facing gate, and on along a field edge past a nearby house and down to the bottom corner.

Turn LEFT along a track past a small pool, then turn RIGHT across a wet tussocky area to the left of the pool to a stile. Go through the small gate ahead and up through trees above the stream and on to a large gate into a field. Follow the fence on your right past a gate and round to another gate in the field corner. Turn LEFT along an enclosed green track, now on a section of the Tegid Way, soon rising past a small wood, then passing a track on the left, to eventually reach Cae-pant farm. Follow its driveway to a road. Follow it RIGHT.

3 After passing a signposted path along the access track to Ty'n-y-fron, take a signposted bridleway angling left along a stony track to a gate and on up to Cae lago. Here turn RIGHT between a wall and a fence to a gate. Continue with the enclosed bridleway to another gate and a stone sheepfold. Go through a gateway ahead and up beside the fence to its corner by a cross-path. Keep ahead, soon descending and continuing to a gate. Go up the track and on across upland pasture to a gate in the boundary corner ahead. (For **Walk B**, turn left and resume text at point 6.)

4 Go through the gate. Ignore the descending track. Instead keep ahead across rough ground past piles of stone, then across upland pasture to join a rising green track ahead to a gate. Keep ahead across the sloping field, then in its corner turn RIGHT through a gate and continue up a green track. After another gate, turn LEFT off the track and follow the wall down to cross a stile by a gate in the continuing fence. Go along the left-hand side of a large reedy marshy area. Just beyond a small lake cross a stile and stream on the right into Open Access land. Turn LEFT up a green quad track, soon bending RIGHT up near a fence. It then bends LEFT with the fence up across the moorland before levelling out at the next fence corner and angling RIGHT to the bottom of the nearby part heather-covered ridge. (Here, a path can be followed up and across the broad ridge – *for all-round views* – soon descending, then bearing left just before a wall corner and descending to the stile at point 5.) The quad track continues beneath the ridge. At the ridge end, about 75 yards before a gate, turn RIGHT along a path to a stile/gate.

5 Follow the wall, then an older wall across the moorland of Mynydd Mynyllod, At its end descend the slope and follow an intermittent path across a wettish area. to go through a gate in the fence on your right about 50 yards before a sheepfold. Continue ahead beside

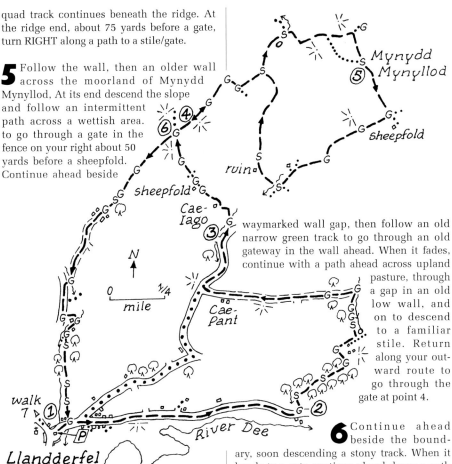

waymarked wall gap, then follow an old narrow green track to go through an old gateway in the wall ahead. When it fades, continue with a path ahead across upland pasture, through a gap in an old low wall, and on to descend to a familiar stile. Return along your outward route to go through the gate at point 4.

6 Continue ahead beside the boundary, soon descending a stony track. When it bends to a gate continue ahead down a path near the boundary to a gate, and on down to another. Cross a nearby stile and follow the permissive path down the field edge to a gate by dwellings. Follow their access track down to a road. Follow it LEFT, past a signposted path, then go through a recessed gate on your left, opposite two on your right. Descend to go through a waymarked gate by a house – *a former mill* – and go along its access track. Just beyond a second house, turn LEFT through iron gates, then RIGHT through a nearby gate. Go along the left-hand edge of a paddock to a stile into a wood. Turn RIGHT and go through the wood edge above the stream and on along the edge of three fields to the road. Turn RIGHT back to the start.

an old embanked boundary, through a gate, and on down the next field. Near the bottom angle LEFT through the boundary and follow a fence to go through a gate in it. Follow the boundary on your left, soon descending a wide path through gorse, then turn LEFT down a narrow green track to join a nearby cottage's access track. Just before a gate and lane, cross a stile up on the right and a fence below. Cross a sleeper bridge and fence ahead, then angle LEFT to a waymarked fence corner. Follow the wall up the slope and after a wall gap near a ruin keep ahead below the fence to a stile in the gorse-covered corner. Continue below the fence. When it bends right, keep ahead to go through a

WALK 7

LLYN MAES Y CLAWDD & EARL'S WOOD

DESCRIPTION A delightful 4½ mile undulating walk from the historic village of Llandderfel in the beautiful Upper Dee valley featuring an ancient church, two small attractive lakes, woodland, and extensive views. The outward route is now a section of the waymarked Tegid Way. The woodland return is known locally as the Queen's Walk, for its association with Queen Victoria's visit to the area in 1889. Allow about 2½ hours.

START Llandderfel [SH 982371].

DIRECTIONS Leave Y Bala on the A494 towards Llangollen, then turn right on the B4401. At a war memorial, turn left into Llanderfel. Take the first road on the right to park alongside a stream opposite the former National School dating from 1828.

*L*landderfel *takes its name from St Derfel Gadarn – Derfel the Mighty – a famous 6thC warrior-saint. The early Christian saints often used the old pagan religion to promote Christianity. St Derfel adopted the same powers as Cernunnos, the god of Nature and the Underworld, who had stag antlers on his head. The church was dedicated to him and many pilgrims came to the village in the Middle Ages to pray to his large wooden image, often bringing animals to be cured and blessed. The tradition that the image would set forests on fire was strangely fulfilled, when in 1538, on the orders of Thomas Cromwell, who wanted to root out superstitious practices, it was removed and publicly burned at Smithfield, London, along with Friar Forest of Greenwich, who was accused of high treason. His wooden stag, without its antlers, which had encouraged pagans to believe that Cernnunos was willing to accept the new religion, is all that remains from the famous shrine and now stands in the church porch. However, it continued to play an important role in village life. Each Easter Tuesday, the 'horse' would be brought out* and carried in procession to a hill near St Derfel's Well. It would then be converted into a ride for local children.

The present church dates from the 15thC. In 1758, the fine oak roof was destroyed by fire. Remnants of it were used in Plas Newydd, the house occupied by the famous 'Ladies of Llangollen'.

Llandderfel is well known for its literary figures. The poet Huw Cae Llwyd visited Rome in 1475 and wrote a famous poem about the relics he saw there, including one which appears very much like the Turin Shroud. Edward Jones, known as 'Barad y Brenin' – the King's Poet – was harpist to the Prince of Wales in 1790. He collected and published many volumes of Welsh music. Other famous sons are R J Berwyn, a radical, who wrote hymns and Welsh periodicals, the 19thC poet Dewi Hafhest, and the local historian Evan Roberts. A slate quarry and the nearby Pale estate provided employment for local people.

Return to the main road in the village. Follow it up past the church and out of the village, then turn LEFT on a road signposted to Cefnddwysarn. It rises steadily, passing Ty-newydd. After ½ mile, when the road bends sharp right, continue ahead up Ty'n-y-bwlch's access track on the waymarked Tegid Way. *After the effort of an early climb, you are rewarded with extensive views, including the Berwyns to the south and the Arans to the west.* Follow the track past Llyn Maes y Clawdd – *a small upland lake, which provides fishing and bird-watching facilities specifically for people with disabilities, following an initiative by the landowners in partnership with statutory and voluntary bodies and the local community. R Williams Parry, when head of Sarnau school in 1913, regularly used to walk past Llyn Maes y Clawdd to visit his sister, who was the minister's wife in Llandderfel. He wrote a poem about his journey, telling of hearing owls hooting in the nearby woods.* After a gate continue along the track passing below the house and descending to go through the right of two facing gates. Continue along the edge of the long field – *with views of distant Llyn Tegid* – and down to a stile in its cor-

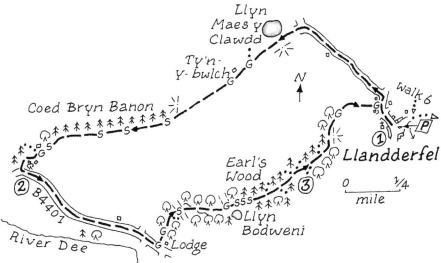

ner. Now follow a stiled field path beneath Coed Bryn Banon down to an old farm. Pass between outbuildings, then continue ahead down its stony access track past the perimeter of a house to the B4401.

2 Cross the road, turn LEFT and follow the attractive valley road past Bod Eryi then the entrance to Llannerch yr Eryr with the river Dee nearby. *In the 1890s, engineers from London came to survey the possibility of making a dam by Bodweni, where the Dee valley is narrow. The resulting lake would have drowned Y Bala. According to the plan, Y Bala would have been rebuilt between Cefn-ddwysarn and Llanderfel!* Shortly take a signposted path through a gate on the left, at the garden corner of Bodweni Lodge to begin the Queen's Walk. Go across the field past a telegraph pole and through a gate ahead by a small wood. Go up the green track for about 40 yards to a waymarked fence corner, then head almost half-LEFT across the field to a waymark post by mature woodland. Join a faint green track above a stream just beyond, soon bending right up to a stile/gate. Turn LEFT down the stony track, then after a few yards turn RIGHT up a waymarked green track alongside a stream through an attractive area of woodland. When the track splits take its left fork across the stream and up through

woodland to an old gateway by attractive Llyn Bodweni. Cross the stony track and continue ahead along the edge of reedy ground parallel with a nearby old fence to a stile in it. Keep ahead along the edge of the wood to another stile and up a field edge to a further stile in the corner into Earl's Wood. Follow a path to the bend of a narrow green track. Keep ahead on a steady descent, then at a track junction turn LEFT on the waymarked path. At the next track junction keep ahead.

3 After a few yards follow the narrow track's right fork down through the trees then along the edge of the wood. Shortly it bends north, becoming a path, which follows a fence past a prominent viewpoint. *Below lies Llandderfel nestling in the part-wooded Dee valley, with the Berwyns beyond. The large house across the valley to your right is Pale Hall, built in 1868 for Henry Robertson, the famous railway engineer, responsible for the impressive Chirk viaduct across the Dee. In 1889, Queen Victoria, with 76 servants, arrived by train at a nearby station for a short stay at Pale. The princes were taken to Ruabon to see a coal mine and travelled on coal trucks lined with velvet!* After a stile at the wood corner follow the initially wide path down the hillside, shortly bending right and continuing down beside a tree boundary then past houses to the road at Llandderfel. Turn RIGHT back to the start.

WALK 8
BWLCH-Y-FENNI & GARTH GOCH

DESCRIPTION A 6¾ mile walk (**A**) exploring an area of upland pasture and forest southeast of Y Bala, with excellent views. The route rises in stages to the ancient high pass of Bwlch-y-Fenni (1385 feet/422 metres), then returns past Creigiau Bwlch. Later it provides views of the old manor house of Plas Rhiwaedog, then visits Garth Goch, the site of the first recorded sheep dog trial. Allow about 4 hours. A shorter 5 mile walk (**B**) is included.

START River bridge, Rhos-y-gwaliau [SH 944346] or by the river in Cwm Hirnant [SH 955337].

DIRECTIONS Take the B4391 south from Y Bala , then turn right on a road signposted to Rhos-y-gwaliau. Go through the hamlet to find limited parking on the no through road by the bridge/river. Alternatively, continue 1 mile along the valley road to a small riverside parking area just past Tyn-y-cwm. (Take a nearby signposted path up through trees and beside the fence to point 2.)

1 Cross the bridge over the river, and just past the side road, take a signposted path on the left. It rises gently across the tree-covered slope above the road, then bends briefly more steeply before continuing up across the higher slope to a stile at the top of the wood. A few yards beyond head half-RIGHT between rock outcrops and across the part tree-covered slope to cross a ladder-stile at a forest corner. Follow the forest perimeter fence to a stile into a field. Continue beside the forest fence to its corner then on to a ladder-stile ahead. Keep ahead, then follow a green track up to a gate. Turn RIGHT alongside the woodland perimeter fence.

2 After 50 yards, at a waymark post, bear LEFT up the slope and through a gap ahead, then bear RIGHT, soon alongside a fence rising towards a forest. At a waymarked post in the fence, about 70 yards below the corner, go half-RIGHT up to a stile in the forest perimeter fence to a path just

beyond. (For **Walk B**, follow the path left along the forest edge, soon descending past a waymark post. Go half-right up a forestry road (a permissive route with the landowner's kind permission). It then contours around the hillside, before descending and bending sharp left. Follow it down to a farm at point 5.)

3 Turn RIGHT and follow the path rising gently through trees, soon joining a green track. Follow it RIGHT soon rising steadily through the replanted forest to a wide forestry road. Follow the waymarked path ahead up an old green track and on to another forestry road. Take a short path opposite to a stile at the forest edge. Go down the field to a gate at the entrance to Maes-hir – *a mid-19thC estate farm*. Turn LEFT to pass between the outbuilding with a clock tower weather vane and the house to a gate. Go up the lane – *once an important route between the Hirnant and the Dee valleys* – to gates and two signposted paths at the high pass of Bwlch-y-Fenni. Take a waymarked path up a green track on the left to go through a gate. Follow the fence on your right to another gate, and on past a forest to cross a stile between gates at the fence corner.

4 Continue with the fence through a new area of conifers. At the fence corner ignore the rising green track, but continue along a bending heather-banked old sunken path past a waymarked path junction and over a stream. The path now descends, soon crossing the bracken-covered eastern slopes of craggy Craigiau y bwlch, loosely parallel with the fence to your right. After a stile in an old gateway, continue ahead, over a stream and on up between rock outcrops, then down upland pasture past a waymark post and on to a stile in the fence ahead. Go half-LEFT across the field and down to a stile at the forest corner. Follow a path down the forest edge, over a green track and on down through conifers to a forestry road. Follow it down towards a farm.

5 Just before the house, cross a stile on the left. Go along the field to a telegraph pole at a boundary corner ahead, then angle

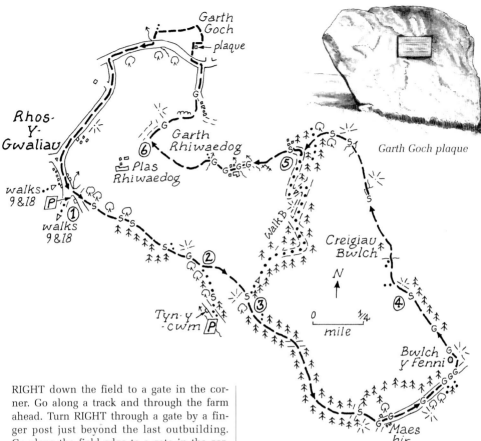

Garth Goch plaque

RIGHT down the field to a gate in the corner. Go along a track and through the farm ahead. Turn RIGHT through a gate by a finger post just beyond the last outbuilding. Go along the field edge to a gate in the corner. Cross a stream and go along the field/wood edge past a stile/gate, then bear LEFT along the bottom slope of Garth Rhiwaedog, round to join a fence on your left. Follow it to a gate by a track leading to nearby Plas Rhiwaedog. *It was the home of Rhivid Flaidd, Lord of Penllyn circa 1160 and later that of the Llwyd family, who rebuilt the hall in the 17thC. It was renowned for its defensive qualities and hospitality to visiting poets, scholars and clergy. In the 18thC, William Jones – a keen nonconformist – accommodated people attending preaching festivals on Y Bala Green each summer. It was said to contain treasures in secret rooms, including a rare relic of Owain Gwynedd – a crystal that turned dull when held in the palm of the hand if a death was imminent – now housed at Rhiwlas.*

6 Ignore the gate, but turn RIGHT and follow a faint green track to another gate. Continue ahead for about 150 yards, then go half-RIGHT down beneath a tree covered rocky ridge. At its end bear LEFT past a farm to a gate in the corner. Follow its driveway down to a road. Cross the road and turn LEFT. At a road sign turn RIGHT across Open Access land to a large boulder on the lower slopes of Garth Goch. *A plaque on it records the first sheep dog trial held on 9th October 1873.* From the boulder follow paths up to boulders on Garth Goch's summit. Immediately after the largest boulder, turn LEFT down a wide path and on across a large flat area. At a cross-path turn LEFT to the road. Turn RIGHT across the bridge over an impressive gorge. Continue up the road, then take a road on the left to Rhos-y-gwaliau.

WALK 9

AROUND CWM HIRNANT & CWM CYMERIG

DESCRIPTION A 5½ mile walk (**A**) exploring the attractive valleys and upland pasture south of Rhos-y-gwaliau, with good views. The route crosses the lower open slopes of Cwm Hirnant, returns to the valley then climbs part tree-covered slopes and crosses upland pasture. After a short rough section of forest it descends to Cwm Cymerig and continues along the wide ridge of Mynydd Cefn-ddwy-Graig, an Open Access area. Allow about 3½ hours. The route includes two easier shorter walks – a 2½ mile walk (**B**) up Cwm Cymerig and along Mynydd Cefn-ddwy-Graig, and a 3 mile walk (**C**) in Cwm Hirnant.

START River bridge, Rhos-y-gwaliau [SH 943346] or Aberhirnant Forestry Commission picnic site/car park, Cwm Hirnant [SH957327]. For the alternative car park continue along the valley road.

DIRECTIONS See Walk 8.

*R*hos-y-Gwaliau *has both a chapel and church. During the 19thC Lady Price of Rhiwlas Hall had churches built at Sarnau, Fron Goch and here to try to encourage tenants back into the Church of England. Llywarch Hen – a 6thC prince of the northern kingdom of Rheged, reputedly invited to Penllyn by a nobleman from Llanfor, is associated with nearby Rhiwaedog. Tradition says he was buried at Llanfor aged 150, having outlived his 24 sons. His last son was reportedly killed in a local battle with the Saxons, who pursued fugitives down the Hirnant.*

I Take the no through road signposted 'Rhos-y-gwaliau Centre' past the Outdoor Education Centre and rising to a junction, just past Cymerig. (For **Walk B**, follow the lane ahead up the attractive Cymerig valley for 1¼ miles. Where the tarmaced lane ends at a gate becoming a track, turn right on a signposted path to rejoin the main route at point 5.) Turn LEFT along the access drive

to Gelli Grin. Go through the farm and a gate just beyond the house. Go up the stony track to a gate, then follow the gated green track across open country – *with good views across the Hirnant valley* – later descending to pass through another farm. Continue down its driveway, shortly passing between dwellings, to the bend of a stony forestry track. Go down the track and on over the Hirnant river to reach the valley road by Aberhirnant Forestry Commission picnic site. (For **Walk C** follow the road left along the scenic wooded river valley back to the start.)

2 Turn RIGHT along the road past Plas Aber-hirnant and Minafon, then take a signposted path through a gate on the right, and across a footbridge over the river. Go up the slope ahead, and after about 70 yards, go half-LEFT up to the waymarked top fence corner of the forest. Cross the forestry track above and go up the slope ahead, over a stony forestry track, and up past an abandoned hillside cottage to cross a stile in the fence by a wood corner. Continue up beside the wood/field boundary to a stile/gate and on to a stony forestry track just above. Follow it RIGHT. Shortly, take a waymarked path on the left up through the trees to rejoin the forestry track. Go up the green track ahead to a stile/gate at the forest edge.

3 Go half-RIGHT to a gate, then continue across upland pasture – *enjoying panoramic views, with Arenig prominent ahead* – soon joining the fence on your left to cross a stile in it. Turn RIGHT for a few yards, then LEFT along a faint narrow green track which heads towards Arenig Fawr, becoming more a sunken path, which gently descends to a wet reedy area. Work your way round to cross a stile in the forest perimeter fence ahead. Go ahead through the cleared/replanted forest and over a stream, following a line of old fence posts by an embankment on your right. Shortly go up on to the embankment to a waymarked post and continue along it. At its end cross a stream and another just ahead. Follow a path for about 40 yards through mixed woodland, with an old wall on your right, to a waymarked path junction by an old lime kiln. Here turn RIGHT and follow a sunken path through a more open forest past a yellow-topped post to a stile into a field.

a nearby ladder-stile/gate across the lane end into Open Access land. Go up the stony track and when it bends right to Gilrhos continue up the narrow green track. Just after it bends right towards a nearby gateway and a small lake beyond, continue on a good path up past rocky outcrops. When it splits

4 Turn LEFT down the field edge past the forest corner and on down the next field edge by the stream past two ruined stone buildings and an entrance into the adjoining field 50 yards below. Continue down the field edge past trees, then before the nearby corner turn LEFT through the tree boundary by a fallen tree. Now follow the left-hand edge of a small triangular reedy field by the stream and embanked tree boundary down to a stile and a nearby yellow-topped post. Cross a sleeper bridge over the stream then go across a field to a stile, and across the next to a gate in front of Gelli-gron cottage. Go through the small waymarked gate ahead above the stream, then turn RIGHT down the field to a gate. Go across the next large field, a green track, then a footbridge over a stream and on to a nearby lane.

5 Continue to a ladder-stile ahead, then follow a path through open woodland, over a stream and on up past a stile to Encil y coed – *a converted 19thC chapel*. Go past the large telegraph pole, then angle RIGHT to

continue with the right fork along the southern edge of the broad ridge of Mynydd Cefn-ddwy-Graig towards two telegraph poles with the fence to your right. After reaching the left telegraph pole, continue with the path from its cable support, taking its right fork to pass another fence corner. Continue beside the fence on a steady descent, then bend LEFT beside a wall down to cross a ladder-stile in its corner.

6 Go down the enclosed path to a gate by an outbuilding. Follow the waymarked path to a small gate below the cottage and down to a kissing gate. It then descends to a then continues down to a green track near a ruin. Follow it down the field to the road at Rhos-y-gwaliau. Turn RIGHT along the road back to the start.

WALK 10

CRAIG YR ALLOR & IS-AFON

DESCRIPTION A 7 mile walk (**A**) exploring the attractive hills south of Y Bala overlooking Llyn Tegid, following good paths and a bridleway. The route rises on good paths to over 1500 feet/470 metres, visits an Open Access viewpoint, passes through a forest then returns with a bridleway across upland pasture and then a section of the waymarked SNP Llyn Tegid trail. Allow about 4 hours. Two described shorter walks of 3½ (**B**) and 2½ (**C**) miles are included. All offer panoramic views.

START Car park at eastern end of Llyn Tegid [SH 928354].

DIRECTIONS From the main street in Y Bala go along Tegid Street opposite the White Lion Royal Hotel. Just beyond the last houses is a car park on the right near Llyn Tegid.

I Follow the pavement along the end of Llyn Tegid – *enjoying superb views along the lake towards the Arans* – to join the B4391. Follow it over where the river Dee emerges from the lake, then cross the old stone bridge and B4403 to the entrance to Bala Lake Railway. Turn LEFT along a path past Ty Penybont – *by the site of a motte and bailey castle*. Continue past the entrance to Pen y Bont touring and camping park, then turn RIGHT on a signposted bridleway along a stony track. After about 70 yards, take a signposted path on the left up through the wood past the bend of a track to a stile at the wood edge.

2 The path rises to a nearby waymarked fence corner and continues below the fence. At its corner, follow it up to a stile. Go half-RIGHT across the field to a stile in the corner. The path continues near the fence to a stile into Open Access land. Go up the slope ahead, then follow a good path across the part gorse-covered terrain and gently descend to a waymarked path junction just before a stile. (For **Walk C**, turn sharp right along a path past gorse, then towards a tele-

graph pole on the skyline to a stile and footbridge. Angle right up a green track onto a small ridge. At a post ahead, bear left to follow the waymarked path down to a ladder-stile at Wenallt, then down the field edge below the house to another ladder-stile. Turn right down the stony access track beyond, past a cottage, then cross a stile on the left. Go half-right, then bear right beneath a small crag above a fence down to stile in it. Go across the field to a stile to the left of a bungalow. (An easier alternative is to follow the waymarked permissive path down the track and through a small gate on the left, past the end of the bungalow to the stile.) Descend through the wood to a track. Turn right to point 6.)

3 Cross the stile and follow the path to a narrow road, with a white cottage – *a former 19thC chapel* – nearby. Follow it RIGHT through open mixed woodland past a track on the left. Shortly, take a waymarked path on the left up through conifers, then turn LEFT up a green track, soon bending right to a ladder-stile/gate. Continue with a faint green track rising across upland pasture near the fence past a stile. (For **Walk B**, cross it and head half-left down the hillside to a stile/finger post and resume text at point 5.) Continue up the track, then at the fence corner above a gate, go half-LEFT to a gate in the fence ahead. Just before it bend LEFT up with the fence for about 50 yards to cross a stile in it. Go up through a narrow reedy cutting and on across open ground for a further 50 yards, then bear LEFT up a distinct sunken path, shortly being joined by a fence on the left to a ladder-stile over it near the fence corner into Open Access land. Follow the good path across the tussocky terrain, later rising to follow the fence on the right up to a ladder-stile. Here, turn LEFT alongside the fence to an initial viewpoint, then head to the highest point, marked by a small pile of stones – *offering panoramic views*. Return along the broad ridge, then head back towards the fence and cross the ladder-stile. Continue up and across the open pasture of Craig yr Allor to a ladder-stile into a forest corner.

4 Follow the waymarked path through the conifers and, at a waymarked path junction keep ahead. At the next waymarked path junction (two posts), turn RIGHT to follow a path down through the forest, later levelling out to reach a waymarked old fence corner in a firebreak. The path now descends again past a yellow topped post and old fence posts, then beside an old embanked boundary to another yellow topped post at its corner. It then bends LEFT down beneath the embanked boundary to an old gateway in it, onto a level bridleway. Follow it RIGHT, soon descending past a waymarked side path then continuing through the forest for ½ mile to eventually leaving it by a gate into Open Access land. The bridleway now contours across the bracken-covered slopes of Is-afon, past a waymarked path, guided by posts, later crossing a stream to a bridle gate. It then continues across the bracken hillside, soon descending and passing below a fence to a bridle gate. I t continues with the fence down to a gate, then down to a stile/finger post below – *offering a panoramic view of Llyn Tegid.*

5 Do not cross the stile. Instead, follow the bridleway down a green track by the fence to a road. Briefly go down the road, then follow the signposted SNP path down across the open hillside towards Y Bala, at a stream turning LEFT down across tussocky, then bracken covered ground to a stile. The path continues down beside a boundary to a cottage, then bends RIGHT up to a waymarked fence end. It now descends steadily beside the old fence, passes a wood corner and continues down a field past a house to a stile. Follow the waymarked path down beneath woodland to a cattle grid on the driveway of nearby former Bala Lake Hotel – *now a holiday centre for John Lewis Partnership staff.* Pass behind the main building, through the rear car park and continue along a track past Rhos Fawr.

6 Soon after passing a signposted path on the right (**Walk B**) cross a stile on the left. Go down two fields and across a footbridge over the Bala Lake railway. Continue to the road beyond to join your outward route.

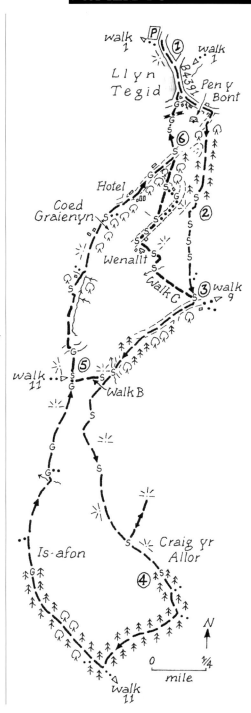

WALK 11

IS-AFON
& CWM GLYN

DESCRIPTION A 6 mile walk (**A**) exploring the hills above Llangower overlooking Llyn Tegid, with great views. The route meanders across lower wooded slopes before rising steadily up Bryniau Goleu. It then follows a bridleway across the open slopes of Is-afon, reaching a height of 1246 feet/ 380 metres, and through a forest before making a stunning descent into Cwm Glyn. Its lower outward and return route follows sections of the SNP Llyn Tegid trail. Allow about 4 hours. The route can be shortened to a 5 mile walk (**B**).
START Snowdonia National Park lakeside car park, Llangower [SH 903321]
DIRECTIONS Follow the B4403 along the south side of Llyn Tegid to Llangower. Go past the church to find the car park and toilets.

Llangower lies on the former turnpike road from Dinas Mawddwy to Y Bala/ Corwen. At its heart was St Cywair's cgurch, now closed. It contained one of the last horse biers to be used in North Wales – reputedly until the late 19thC – 18ft in length, it was strung between horses to carry coffins. In the churchyard is an ancient yew tree. The narrow gauge steam railway runs for 4½ miles from Llanuwchllyn along Llyn Tegid on the trackbed of the former Ruabon – Barmouth Railway line, which closed in 1965.

I Walk back along the road past the church, a side road and telephone box, then take a no through road on the right. Follow it up the attractive lower wooded Glyn valley. Shortly, do a sharp U-turn LEFT on the signposted SNP path up a stony track, past farm buildings and up towards a house. The path passes behind the house and through a gate beyond, then continues alongside the fence up through a large then small gate. Follow the fence across the tree-covered hillside to a finger post. Descend a nearby stream guided by yellow topped posts. After about 120 yards cross it, then angle LEFT down to cross a stile, a footbridge over a stream, and

stile beyond. Continue beside the fence, later passing a ladder-stile. Soon the path begins a steady climb up Brynau Goleu to a stile at a great viewpoint onto a bridleway.

2 Turn RIGHT up alongside the fence to a gate. The bridleway continues near the fence up to a bridle gate, passes below a fence then continues up and across the bracken covered hillside to another bridle gate. After crossing a stream the bridleway contours across the western slopes of Is-afon guided by white-topped posts, past a way-marked side path, to a gate into the forest. Follow the bridleway through the initially closed then more open forest. After about ½ mile you reach a waymarked side path. (For **Walk B**, follow it down through the trees to a forestry track. Turn right, then follow the nearby waymarked path left down through the trees to a narrow road. Follow it down Cwm Glyn to rejoin the main route at point 4.) Continue with the waymarked bridleway, through an old gateway and on through the forest, over a stream and past a ruined cottage. In a clearing beyond descend an old track to join a wide stony forestry track. Follow it LEFT to a junction of tracks.

3 Go half-RIGHT up the middle track. At a building turn RIGHT and at the gated entrance to Ffridd Bach cottage, turn LEFT to pass behind it and on through a short section of trees to a waymark post. Turn LEFT up the bridleway through the open forest to cross a stream. At a waymarked path/bridleway junction beyond, turn RIGHT and follow the path through the forest down to a stile at its edge. Go through a gap in the fence ahead, then ahead down reedy terrain to walk along the left-hand side of a line of trees. At its end cross a stream, pass through reeds and continue with a path along another line of trees to a water storage tank. Follow an old sunken tree-lined path down towards Cae'r-hafotty. Just before the house turn RIGHT down through trees, then LEFT past out-buildings. Continue along its delightful high-level access track – *enjoying stunning views* – shortly meandering down the hillside and passing a ruin. Just before two cottages turn RIGHT alongside an old wall and follow the waymarked sunken path down above the Afon Glyn to a road by a converted 19thC chapel. Follow it ahead.

4 Soon after passing the side road, turn sharp LEFT on the signposted SNP path down to cross the concrete bridge over

walk 10 take a no through road on the right. Follow it up the valley, then take another narrow road angling left up across the wooded slope. It rises steadily above the river and eventually becomes a stony track, soon joining a wider stony forestry track. Follow it ahead to a junction of tracks. Now follow instructions from paragraph 3 of Walk 11.

the river. Go up the forestry track. On its bend, take the signposted path ahead to a stile, then up a tree-lined section to another stile. Follow the path over further stiles to Ty-cerig farm. Turn LEFT through a gate and up the slope to a finger post and on up to a stile on the skyline. Go across the field – *enjoying extensive views of Llyn Tegid* – then down to a footbridge over a stream in a narrow dingle. At the top turn RIGHT down a faint narrow green track by the dingle to a road. Follow it down into Llangower and back to the start.

WALK 12
CWM GLYN

DESCRIPTION A 4¾ mile walk up an attractive wooded side valley on narrow roads then a bridleway/forestry tracks, reaching a height of about 1345 feet/410 metres, before making a stunning descent, with great views. Allow about 3 hours.
START As Walk 11.

I Walk back along the road past the church, a side road and a telephone box, then

The former church at Llangower

WALK 13

CWM CYNLLWYD

DESCRIPTION A well waymarked 6 mile walk (**A**) exploring both sides of attractive Cwm Cynllwyd. The route initially follows the Aran ridge path before heading along the valley to the remote farming community of Talardd. It then climbs steeply, reaching 1214 ft/370 metres with stunning views of the Aran ridge, to Bryn Melyn, before descending wild Cwm Fechan to ford the river (route **a**). An alternative, especially when the river is high, is to continue along a new scenic high level waymarked SNP permissive path (route **b**), then road to Llanuwchllyn. Allow about 4 hours. A shorter 3 mile walk (**B**) is included.

START Snowdonia National Park car park, Llanuwchllyn [SH 880298].

DIRECTIONS The car park lies on the B4403 at the southern end of Llanuwchllyn just before the bridge over the river.

I From the bend near the bridge follow the signposted Aran Ridge path up the no through road, then after 1/3 mile over a ladder-stile on the right and up to another ladder-stile. Continue up the bridleway past a ladder-stile to a ladder-stile/gate ahead. The bridleway continues to rise. At a waymark post, take the left fork (the Aran ridge path) up the hillside. After a ladder-stile, keep alongside the fence. Just before the path begins to descend, divert to the nearby cairned top of Garth Fawr for extensive views, then continue down the main path. At a ladder-stile in the fence and just before a ladder-stile/ wall ahead, turn LEFT across tussocky pasture to a stile in the fence ahead. Turn LEFT over a stream, then RIGHT to follow a faint path across the slope ahead to a waymark post. Descend the slope to a waymarked section of wall into a wood. Angle RIGHT to a stile and on to a waymark post ahead. Go half-LEFT down the large field, across a reedy area to a stile in the bottom fence. Go down the next field to a gate in the corner near a large barn at Plas Morgan. *The mansion, now demolished, was once occupied by Peter Price – the son of a buccaneer on the Spanish Main.* Turn LEFT down the

track past the end of the barn to a waymark post just after it bends left. (For **Walk B** simply follow the track/road back to the start.)

2 Turn RIGHT down the field edge, over a stream, to a stile/gate. Turn RIGHT up the field edge to cross a stile. Turn LEFT briefly along the green track, then keep ahead across a reedy area and go across the middle of the large field to a stile into a small wooded dingle. The path now crosses three streams then a stile, and continues up to a yellow-topped post on the skyline. It continues across the large reedy area past another post to a stile/gate. After a stream and a small gate, continue ahead to a stile/gate by a farm. Go past the front of the house, through a gate ahead and pass to the right of a stone barn up to a ladder-stile. Continue up to another ladder-stile ahead, then follow the waymarked path along the bottom edge of the large field.

3 At the waymarked fence corner, continue across the field to a ladder-stile. Angle slightly RIGHT up the next field to a ladder-stile/ gate by trees. Follow the waymarked path along the next field edge down to go through a metal gate. Follow the waymarked permissive path past outbuildings and down a gated stony track to pass the front of Tyn-y-Cae. Just before a gate turn LEFT down the field edge to a gate in the corner to join the nearby road in the attractive side valley of Cwm Croes. (Alternatively continue down the stony track.) Follow the road to Talardd, crossing a confluence of rivers, then passing a chapel to reach a road junction. *This tiny community, situated at the junction of ancient routes, once boasted two chapels.*

4 Turn RIGHT, and at the telephone box, take the signposted path angling up to a gate. The waymarked path passes behind a house and rises to a gap in the tree boundary, then climbs steeply beside it to a green track. From the nearby waymark post take a path angling LEFT up the slope to a stile/ old gate. Continue in the same direction up the hillside to a stile/gateway at the highest point of the walk – *with extensive views of the Arans.* Go across the next field to a stile/ gate, then continue across the edge of reedy

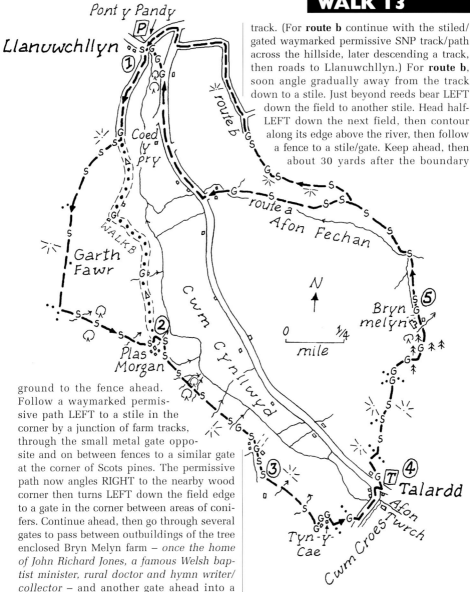

track. (For **route b** continue with the stiled/gated waymarked permissive SNP track/path across the hillside, later descending a track, then roads to Llanuwchllyn.) For **route b**, soon angle gradually away from the track down to a stile. Just beyond reeds bear LEFT down the field to another stile. Head half-LEFT down the next field, then contour along its edge above the river, then follow a fence to a stile/gate. Keep ahead, then about 30 yards after the boundary

ground to the fence ahead. Follow a waymarked permissive path LEFT to a stile in the corner by a junction of farm tracks, through the small metal gate opposite and on between fences to a similar gate at the corner of Scots pines. The permissive path now angles RIGHT to the nearby wood corner then turns LEFT down the field edge to a gate in the corner between areas of conifers. Continue ahead, then go through several gates to pass between outbuildings of the tree enclosed Bryn Melyn farm – *once the home of John Richard Jones, a famous Welsh baptist minister, rural doctor and hymn writer/collector* – and another gate ahead into a field. Go down its edge to cross a ladder-stile.

5 Follow the well waymarked path down the reedy field to a cross a stile and a new footbridge over the Afon Fechan in the wild upland valley. Turn LEFT then at a second post turn RIGHT up the waymarked path to a stile, then along the old reedy track to another stile/ gate. Continue along the reedy

end, the path angles left down to a gate near the river. Cross it at a ford downstream, go through the farm and along its access track to the road. Turn RIGHT. Follow the road for just over ½ mile. Just below Pen-rhiw-dwrch, take a signposted path through a small gate on the right. Descend steps and follow a path angling down above a wooded valley through kissing gates to reach Pont-y-Pandy bridge.

WALK 14

CASTELL CARNDOCHAN & CWM LLIW

DESCRIPTION A 5½ mile walk exploring both sides of the lower Lliw valley, with extensive views and featuring an early climb (optional) to an impressive remote ancient hilltop castle (1115 feet/340 metres), accessible in Open Access land, offering extensive views. Afterwards the route follows a bridleway into attractive open upland country, then down to cross the Afon Lliw. After passing through Coed Wenallt, the route rises up the other side of the valley to follow a scenic high-level road, before returning mostly by field paths. Allow about 3½ hours. The route can be undertaken as two shorter walks of 3 miles and 2¾ miles by utilising the linking section of road from and to point 3.
START Pont Dolhendre [SH 853308].
DIRECTIONS From Y Bala follow the A494 past Llyn Tegid, then just before Llanuwchllyn, turn right along a road signposted to Trawsfynydd. After about 1½ miles you reach a telephone & post box by a bridge over the river (Pont Dolhendre), where there is limited roadside parking.

*C*astell Carndochan – a ridge top castle probably built by Llywelyn ap Iorwerth in the early 13thC. It contained a round tower at its northern end, a D-shaped one to the south, and a square building in the centre. In those days Penllyn belonged to Powys. Llywelyn later annexed Penllyn and it became part of Gwynedd. For a few generations, the noblemen of Penllyn still chose to be buried in Powys. Near the castle was a gold mine, once owned by John Bright, a Quaker MP, which was worked between 1860–1910.

1 Cross the bridge over the Afon Lliw and walk up the road. At cross-roads, turn RIGHT and follow the road up to its end at Tanycastell, then continue up the stony access track beneath Castell Carndochan, soon levelling out. Just before the track bends

over a stream, go through the first gate up to your left below a small stone building. Follow an old track up across the hillside, later bending sharp left then disappearing in reeds. Briefly continue in the same direction towards the craggy top of Castell Carndochan then angle up onto the high ground to your right and continue to the distinctive rocky hilltop castle. Retrace your steps then just below in a small depression full of stones take a clear path on the right descending north-west. It soon angles down across the initially boulder-covered slope, then levels out. Descend to the end of a fence below to rejoin the outward track down to the gate and the stony access track.

2 Follow the stony track across the stream and up through the forest, over a cattle grid, then up across open pasture – *with Moel Llyfnant and Arenig Fawr prominent ahead* – to eventually reach the gated entrance to a house. Go through the small gate to its right, then pass to the right of a waymarked bridleway telegraph pole to a large gate ahead. Go half-RIGHT across the next field and through a gap in an old low wall just to the right of a tree, then angle RIGHT down to go through a gate in the wall corner. Follow the boundary on your left then go through a small metal gate ahead. Continue ahead down the steep slope, soon by the fence, to a gate and across a large footbridge over the Afon Lliw below. Go through trees to a forestry track and follow it RIGHT through Coed Wenallt, soon bending away from the river. After passing an open aspect looking towards Castell Carndochan, take a rough stony track angling down on the right through trees, marked by blue banded white poles. At a pole on the left bend RIGHT down a narrowing path to a small gate into Dolhendre Uchaf caravan park. Follow the track head through the site to an entrance gate onto a road. Continue ahead along the road.

3 At the next caravan park entrance go through a set of wooden gates opposite into a field. Go half-RIGHT to the second of two gates and across the middle of the next field to cross a small river and on through a

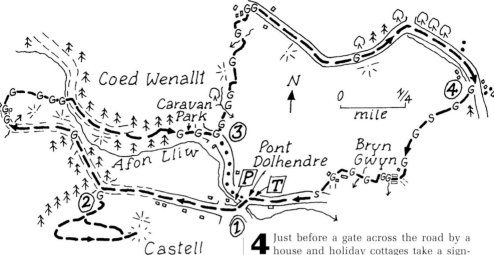

Coed Wenallt

Caravan Park ③

Afon Lliw

Castell Carndochan

②

①

Pont Dolhendre

Bryn Gwyn

④

N

0   ¼
mile

P   T

gate ahead. Go up the stony track to the small quarry hole, then turn LEFT to a nearby gate into a field. Walk towards a telegraph post ahead. Here turn RIGHT up an old boundary and after about 40 yards turn LEFT through a sunken gap, and up the next field to a gate in the fence. Now follow a narrow rising sunken green track, shortly bending left to a stream and a gate, where it ends. Continue ahead, then after about 50 yards angle RIGHT up towards a farm. Follow a gated track up round its outbuildings, then turn sharp RIGHT up its stony access track to a gate. Just beyond it becomes a narrow road and passes Brynllech Isaf, then rises before steadily descending – *offering panoramic views*. It levels out and passes a forest, then begins a long steady descent, soon passing a house.

4 Just before a gate across the road by a house and holiday cottages take a sign-posted path angling RIGHT to a nearby gate. Go across the field and through a waymarked gate in the corner. Follow the tree boundary on your right to cross a stile in the field's reedy corner. Now head half-LEFT down to go through a metal gate in the corner. Follow the boundary on your right, soon descending towards a Bryn Gwyn farm to a gate. Continue down a rough track, then at Bryn Gwyn's access track turn RIGHT through the farmyard. Pass between the house and outbuildings to a gate and another one ahead by a small wood. Follow the boundary on the left round to a gate in the field corner. Don't go through it but turn RIGHT along the field edge on a waymarked path to a gate in the other corner. Follow a faint green track over a stream and through another gate by a farm outbuilding. Follow the waymarked path past the farm and down a stony track to a gate. At more outbuildings, where the track bends left continue ahead down the field to a stile onto a road. Follow it RIGHT back to the start.

Castell Carndochan

WALK 15

PARC

DESCRIPTION A 4¾ mile (**A**) or 2¾ (**B**) walk exploring the countryside near the historic community of Parc on waymarked paths and quiet roads. The route follows field paths to join the Snowdonia National Park Authority northern section of the Llyn Tegid trail, which it follows east to Llwyn-mawr-isaf farm. Here Walk B returns along a recently upgraded section of field paths. Walk A rises to a good viewpoint then continues further east with the trail, before returning by quiet scenic upland road and field paths. Allow about 3 hours.

START Parc [SH 877339].

DIRECTIONS Take the A494 out of Y Bala towards Dolgellau, and after about 3½ miles, just past Glanllyn Caravan and Camping Park, turn right to follow the road signposted to Parc. Descend into the village and go across a bridge over the river to park tidily on the roadside.

*P*arc *is a small community named after the area's historical association as a hunting park, where the Burgesses of Y Bala exercised their rights to hunt, given to them at the establishment of the town. It is known as the birthplace of Merched y Wawr – a Welsh-speaking organisation for women in Wales, with about 280 local branches. It was established in 1967 by the Parc branch of the long established Women's Institute after the WI controversially insisted on English as the official language. The area is also important for Welsh penillion singing (singing poetry in counterpoint to a traditional melody).*

I Cross the bridge over the river and take the first turning on the left by Hen Bost opposite the former school, which closed in 2013 despite much local opposition, but is now the Community Centre. Follow the access track to Rhyd yr Efael farm, taking its right fork up to the house and down to a waymarked gate just below. Keep ahead, and at the fence corner angle LEFT across the field, over a stream by a reedy area and on to cross another by a waymarked fence corner. Continue alongside the fence to cross a footbridge over the stream and stiles into a field. Turn RIGHT and follow the signposted path across the middle of the field, through a gap in the boundary at a stream and on across the next field to cross another stream. Now follow the signposted path up the next field with the outbuildings at Plas Madog – *an old manor house* – below and on to a stile/gate onto a road.

2 Go through the gate opposite and head across the field to a waymarked gate. Continue across the next field to cross a stile/sleeper bridge, then turn LEFT. At the fence corner keep ahead – *with good views of Llyn Tegid* – to cross a stile in the corner and a stream. Now head half-RIGHT across a large field towards the Arans to go through a waymarked gateway near the corner and on to reach a nearby stony access track by a finger post, where you join the SNP Llyn Tegid trail.

3 Turn LEFT down the track to the road by cottages. Turn LEFT along the road, then follow the SNP trail along a long driveway on the right, briefly near the river, to Llwyn-mawr-isaf. Follow a track past the house to a ladder-stile on the right just beyond the last outbuilding. (For **Walk B** continue along the access track to a gate at nearby Llwyn-mawr-canol farm. Follow the waymarked path through two gates passing to the left of the house, then across a field to another gate. Turn LEFT along the field edge to a small gate. Go across the field to a gate by a finger post then descend the next field to a footbridge over a stream and a gate into the adjoining field. Turn LEFT along the field edge to a gate by Dol Llychwyn. Turn RIGHT along its driveway, past Dolgoed, then just before it reaches a road follow the short gated path on the left by the river to the road bridge. Follow the road left into Parc.)

4 Cross the ladder-stile and go up the steep field edge to a ladder-stile. Go half-LEFT up the next field – *soon with a good view of Llyn Tegid and the Arans* – to a ladder-stile in the corner. Bear LEFT to follow a track towards Llwyn-mawr-uchaf farm. Just before outbuildings angle RIGHT to a ladder-stile ahead by a telegraph pole. Continue beside the garden boundary then go to a stile ahead. Go through the long field to a ladder-stile, then along the edge of the next to a stile. Go along the next field then before the corner cross a stile on the right into the adjoining field. Continue along its edge to a ladder-stile, then the edge of the next field to a stile and across a further field to a stile/

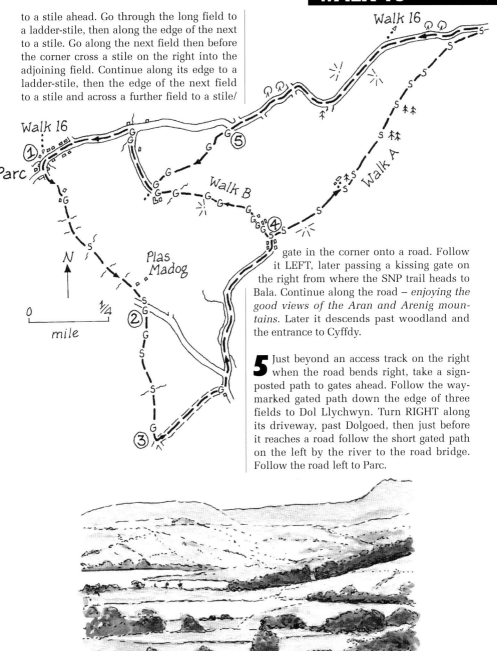

gate in the corner onto a road. Follow it LEFT, later passing a kissing gate on the right from where the SNP trail heads to Bala. Continue along the road – *enjoying the good views of the Aran and Arenig mountains.* Later it descends past woodland and the entrance to Cyffdy.

5 Just beyond an access track on the right when the road bends right, take a sign-posted path to gates ahead. Follow the way-marked gated path down the edge of three fields to Dol Llychwyn. Turn RIGHT along its driveway, past Dolgoed, then just before it reaches a road follow the short gated path on the left by the river to the road bridge. Follow the road left to Parc.

View towards Llyn Tegid and the Arans

WALK 16

MOEL Y GARNEDD (1)

DESCRIPTION A 5 mile walk featuring the area's most prominent viewpoint. The route heads east on paths and a quiet scenic country road, then crosses Open Access heathland, before heading uphill to the summit of Moel y Garnedd (1180 feet)/360 metres) for panoramic all-round views. It then descends and heads west on intermittent paths across featureless and largely reedy tussocky moorland, before returning across farmland. The route is for experienced hill walkers and should be avoided in poor visibility. Allow about 3½ hours.
START Parc [SH 877339].
DIRECTIONS See Walk 15.

1 Continue along the road through the village past the side road to Arenig. Immediately after crossing a bridge over a river take a short signposted gated path on the right, then follow the access road past Dolgoed to Dol Llychwyn at a junction of paths. At the end of the tarmac go through the first waymarked gate immediately on the left. Follow the waymarked path up the edge of three fields to rejoin the road. Follow it for just over ½ mile, then take a signposted Snowdonia National Park path through a kissing gate on the left. Go along the field edge past a small plantation, at its corner bending left to cross a stile into Open Access land and a footbridge beyond. Head half-RIGHT across the heathland below Moel y Garnedd, with its summit trig point initially visible, on an improving path, later passing a finger post. *The heathland, known as Gwastadros, is Common Land, which has provided rough grazing for animals for generations.*

2 Just before a ladder-stile/gate by trees hiding the nearby cottage of Ty'n-y-rhos, turn LEFT across the tussocky ground to a path on high ground ahead and continue up the southern slope of Moel y Garnedd to the trig point on its broad summit. Turn LEFT

a few yards to the west, then go half-RIGHT down its western slope towards Arenig Fawr, passing between a small reedy area and the slope on your right, where there is a cross path, and on down the hillside, soon joining a clear path descending its lower slope. From the bottom of the slope the path continues towards the summit of Arenig Fawr. After about 100 yards at a small area of gorse the path splits. Take its right fork and when it fades continue towards Arenig Fawr's summit across more tussocky/reedy terrain on a long gentle decent, later crossing a stream and following a sketchy path to a stile in the fence by an old gate, marked by a yellow-topped post.

3 Cross a stream just ahead, then angle RIGHT past a small tree and across tussocky ground to join an old embanked boundary by another tree. It bends left and soon descends past a joining tree boundary. At the embanked boundary corner go half-LEFT across a field to a fence corner and descend to a track below. Follow the track over the adjoining stream and up, soon enclosed by boundaries, to an old farm. Turn LEFT to a stile/gate onto a road. Follow it LEFT.

4 After crossing the Afon Isaf, cross a stile on the left and follow the left of two signposted stiled paths through the edge of three fields above the wooded river. After a gate continue through two further fields (gates) towards the Arans, then follow the boundary on your right through the next to a gate in the corner and one ahead. Follow an initially reedy but improving track down to Argoed farm. Bend right through the farmyard between outbuildings, then angle RIGHT to an old gate. Go across the field edge to a sleeper bridge/stile, then almost half-LEFT across the next field to a ladder-stile onto a road. Turn RIGHT then cross a stile on the left just before a nearby farm. Go down the field to a gate, then slightly right across the next field towards Parc to follow an enclosed stiled path between dwellings to the village road.

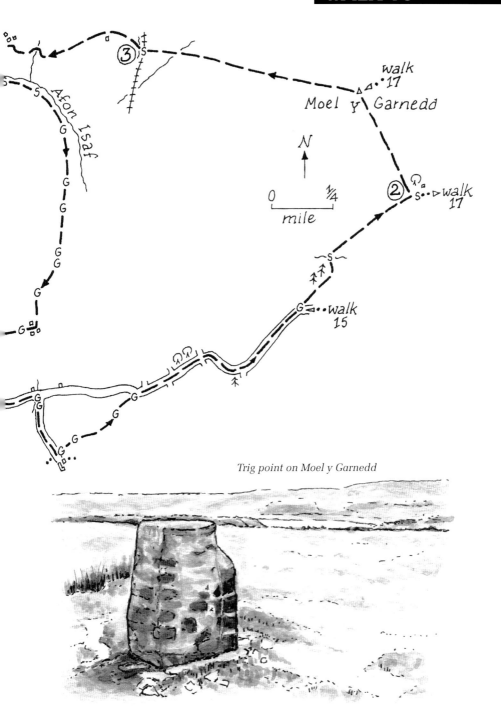

Afon Isaf

walk 17

Moel y Garnedd

N

0   ¼
mile

② s ▷ walk 17

walk 15

Trig point on Moel y Garnedd

MOEL Y GARNEDD (2)

DESCRIPTION A 3¾ mile (**A**) walk from Llanycil to one of the area's most prominent viewpoints. The route rises in stages with a bridleway up to Open Access moorland then follows paths to the summit of Moel y Garnedd (1180 feet)/360 metres). It then descends its southern slope and returns along the waymarked SNP Llyn Tegid trail. Allow about 2½ hours. *The route is for experienced walkers and should be avoided in poor visibility.* Lower 2¾ (**B**) and 1¾ (**C**) mile walks are included.
START A494 lay-by, Llanycil [SH 914349]
DIRECTIONS The lay-by is near the side road to Parc, opposite the former church.

L lanycil church is now a heritage cen-tre celebrating the story of 15-year-old Mary Jones who, in 1800, walked 26 miles barefoot to Y Bala to buy a Bible, leading to the launch of the Bible Society. Betsi Cadwaladr (1789–1860), a renowned nurse with Florence Nightingale in the Crimean War, was christened here.

right of a short tree boundary, then bends left along the adjoining field edge to a gate, and goes along a hedge-lined track to a gate at Penlan farm. (For **Walk C**, go through the adjoining gate, and turn right across two fields, and down to a finger post to join the returning route.)

2 Follow the bridleway through the farm and along its access road. On its bend go through the waymarked gate ahead into Open Access land and along a short narrow green track. At its end continue ahead along a quad bike track. Just beyond small trees bend sharp LEFT past a small gate in the nearby fence. At its corner, bear RIGHT to follow a good path, initially near the fence, then roughly parallel with it. As it begins to rise and splits, follow the path ahead to pass just to the right of a group of five trees, then bend LEFT behind them to a crossroad of paths. (For **Walk B**, follow the path ahead down past a rock outcrop to a ladder-stile/gate by a tree. Go to a gate in the right-hand field corner into the caravan park. Turn right along its access road round to the site entrance. Go down the driveway to point 4.)

1 Cross to the pavement opposite and fol-low it east past the churchyard, then cross the road and go through Fron Feuno Farm's entrance. Follow the waymarked bridleway up the stony track, then after 75 yards half-RIGHT to a small gate and up through the wood to another and on to a waymarked large gate. It then follows a rough track up past Fron Feuno, and con-tinues up the now green track. At a waymark post, the bridleway angles LEFT and follows the nearby fence to a gate. It continues to the

3 Turn RIGHT up the path and in a slight hollow the clear path heads half-LEFT and continues up across moorland, passing close to a small tree then a fence/wall cor-ner. Continue up the path then bear LEFT beneath a small rocky escarpment. After 20 yards, at gorse, go half-RIGHT to join a clear path rising across the broad top of Moel y

Garnedd to a trig point offering panoramic views. From its south side follow a path heading down the hillside to eventually cross a ladder-stile beyond the right-hand end of lower trees hiding Ty'n-y-rhos cottage. Go past the cottage, over its access track and across the large field to a ladder-stile/gate. Follow a green track to a farm and cross a nearby ladder-stile. Go up the field edge to a ladder-stile then turn RIGHT to a ladder-stile ahead. Follow a stiled path across two fields into Bala Caravan Park. Follow a short lane past a house to cross the main driveway.

4 Go past the Information/Games room, then between cottages to a gate. Go across the field to a small gate, then slightly left down the next to another gate and a footbridge below. Go up the field to a finger post by the boundary. Turn RIGHT down a path, and as it rises half-left continue ahead down the edge of the long field to a stile, then follow the path through the wood down to another stile. The waymarked path descends the slope ahead and continues to Fron Feuno Farm's access track. Follow it down to join your outward route.

WALK 18
MYNYDD CEFN-DDWY-GRAIG

DESCRIPTION A short but rewarding 2¼ mile walk exploring the small Open Access hill of Mynydd Cefn-ddwy-graig (1142 ft/348 metres), with a small lake and a panoramic viewpoint, south of Y Bala. Allow about 2 hours.
START River bridge, Rhos-y-gwaliau [SH 944346].
DIRECTIONS See Walk 8.

I Continue up the road past the Outdoor Education Centre, then take a signposted path through a small gate on the right. Follow the path across the sloping field to another small gate. The waymarked path soon passes beneath a large stone house,

continues by the river, then rises through woodland above small falls to a small gate. It continues across the bracken-covered slope to a stile, then rises steadily across the rocky/bracken covered hillside of Mynydd Cefn-ddwy-graig, shortly bending right more steeply. Soon, look for a path leading more left to a nearby short wall. Follow it to its end and a nearby stile. Go up to another stile, then follow the fence on the left past outbuildings below and close to an old cottage. Follow its green access track, then take a rougher green track on the left.

2 As it heads towards a small lake go slightly right to join another green track. It passes through two gateways and continues to a stony track at the entrance to Gilrhos. Turn RIGHT along a green track, shortly bending east – *with a view of Y Bala* – and descending towards a gate. Just before it turn RIGHT up a path. Now follow paths across upland pasture roughly parallel with the fence below to pass below a telegraph pole. Continue towards a distant white house, soon descending a narrow green track to the boundary wall. Follow it LEFT to a ladder-stile. Go down the enclosed path to a gate by an outbuilding. Follow the waymarked path ahead, passing below the cottage to a small gate and down to a kissing gate, then to a small gate. Continue down to a waymark post near a ruin, then a green track down the field ahead to the road in Rhos-y-gwaliau. Turn RIGHT back to the start.

WALK 19
TRYWERYN TRAIL

DESCRIPTION A delightful 1½ mile way-marked riverside nature trail along the international renowned wooded white water stretch of the Trywern to the fish trap below Llyn Celyn reservoir. A more detailed Trail booklet is available from the Centre (Sandy Buttle building), which has a cafe. Allow about an hour. Note that the river level can rise rapidly when water is released from the dam above, so heed the warning signs.

START Canolfan Trywern – The National Whitewater Centre [SH 892401].

DIRECTIONS Canolfan Trywern lies just off the A4212. Y Bala-Trawsfynydd road, about 4 miles from Y Bala. Use the main car park beyond the Centre.

In the 1960s there occurred a sad chapter in modern Welsh history, when the Welsh speaking community of Capel Celyn, with its cottages, farms, school, chapel and churchyard, despite national protests, was drowned by Liverpool City Corporation to create the reservoir of Llyn Celyn. One of the unexpected consequences of controlled releases of water into the Afon Trywern down to the Dee, has been the development of the river for kayaking and canoeing since the mid 1970s. It has has pioneered whitewater rafting in the UK and hosted international competitions and world championships.

From the centre of the car park, take the signposted Trywern Trail under the former railway line, across a footbridge over the river, through a small island to another footbridge. Continue on the waymarked riverside trail to the Celyn Fish Trap. Turn RIGHT along its access road. At a junction turn RIGHT, then go through a gate on the right by waymark 16. Follow the green track through trees to another gate. Briefly rejoin your outward route, then continue on a higher stony track, passing between buildings, to reach the main car park. From its entrance follow the riverside trail to cross a nearby bridge over the river. Continue with the trail past the bend in the river by the Centre opposite – *known as 'The Elbow' from its shape and what you bang when things go wrong!* The trail continues near the former Bala-Ffestiniog railway line. *Opened in 1882, and extended to Blaenau in 1883, it carried passengers and freight, especially slate from the nearby Arenig quarries, until its closure in 1961.* Shortly, cross the footbridge over the river and follow the stony riverside trail to the Centre, then roadside paths to the car park.

WALK 20
CRAIG Y GARN

DESCRIPTION A 3¾ mile walk (**A**) featuring a short section of the Tryweryn Trail, and the craggy top of Craig y Garn (1512 feet/461 metres), now an Open Access area, offering extensive all-round views. The route follows the riverside trail, then rises in stages to the base of Craig y Garn, before making a short ascent to its summit, returning to cross the Afon Hesgyn and following field paths to rejoin the outward route. The ascent up Craig y Garn can be omitted, making a 3 mile walk (**B**). The walk can also be extended to incorporate the remainder of the Tryweryn Trail.

START Canolfan Tryweryn - as Walk 19.

From the car park entrance follow the waymarked riverside trail to cross the nearby bridge over the river. Continue with the riverside trail, passing the Centre opposite, and soon near the former Bala-Ffestiniog railway line. Cross the footbridge over the river to the rafting car park entrance and go to the nearby A4212. Turn RIGHT along the road edge with care, soon passing a former chapel. After a further 150 yards go up a narrow gated access road opposite. At Efrog Newydd cottage, turn RIGHT on a waymarked path up to a shed. Continue up the tree-lined path to cross a stile and a stream just beyond. Follow the right bank of the stream up to another stile/gateway. Continue ahead through a reedy area to a Tir Gorfal access map by gorse to join a track beyond. It rises steadily near the stream – *offering a*

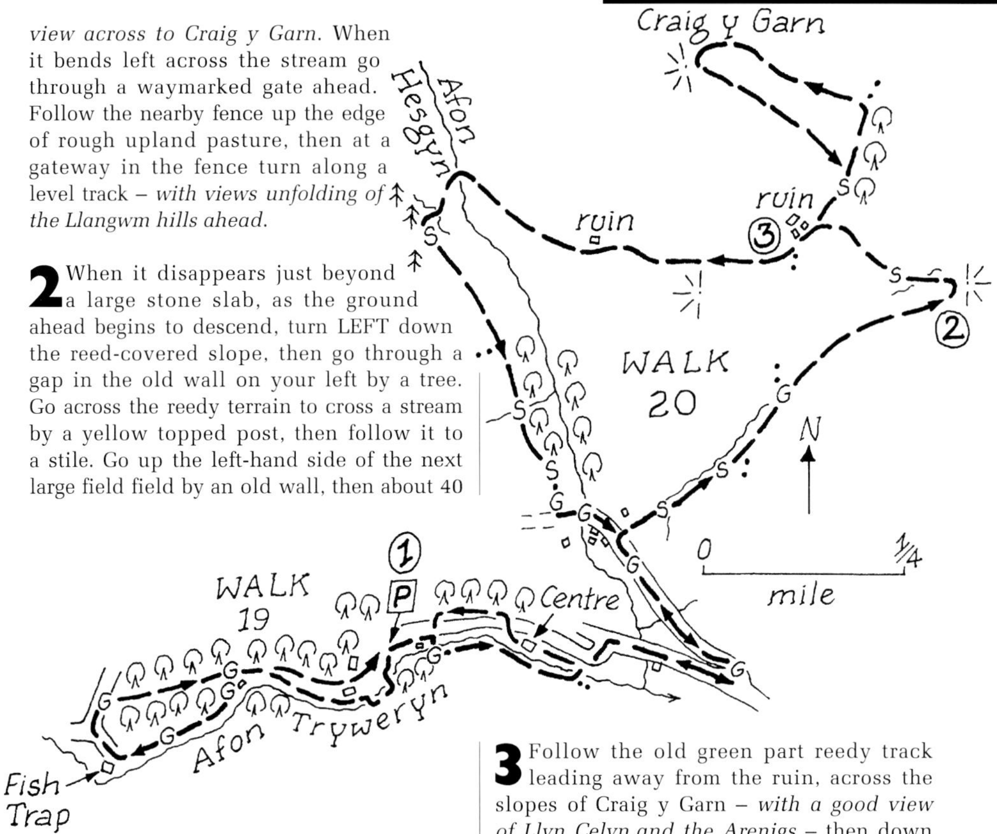
Craig y Garn
Afon Hesgyn
ruin
ruin
3
2
WALK
20
N
0
1/4
mile
1
P
WALK
19
Centre
Afon Tryweryn
Fish Trap

view across to Craig y Garn. When it bends left across the stream go through a waymarked gate ahead. Follow the nearby fence up the edge of rough upland pasture, then at a gateway in the fence turn along a level track – *with views unfolding of the Llangwm hills ahead.*

2 When it disappears just beyond a large stone slab, as the ground ahead begins to descend, turn LEFT down the reed-covered slope, then go through a gap in the old wall on your left by a tree. Go across the reedy terrain to cross a stream by a yellow topped post, then follow it to a stile. Go up the left-hand side of the next large field field by an old wall, then about 40 yards before its corner, go through a wall gap and angle up to cross a wall by the remains of an upland farm. (For **Walk B** resume text at point 3.) Turn RIGHT and follow the boundary up to a stile by a gate to enter Open Access land. Just above bear RIGHT on a path which rises past a small wood. When opposite a gate at the wood corner, turn LEFT and follow a path up the slope. After levelling out the path rises half-LEFT to pass beneath crags onto the top of Craig y Garn just north of its highest point. *From its summit cairn and nearby large rock with a memorial slate, are great views of Llyn Celyn, the Arenigs and the Arans.* Either descend the same way or go onto the adjoining high crags, then work your way down the south-eastern slopes to the right-hand wood corner to return to the ruin.

3 Follow the old green part reedy track leading away from the ruin, across the slopes of Craig y Garn – *with a good view of Llyn Celyn.and the Arenigs* – then down to pass in front of a ruined house and on to another small ruin. Now follow a good path down to cross stiles and a footbridge over the Afon Hesgyn. Turn LEFT up an old green track, then follow a stream up to the small plantation above. Here turn LEFT to cross a nearby stile and go down the edge of a large field, shortly accompanied by a nearby fence, to cross a ladder-stile and footbridge in the bottom corner. Follow the field/wood boundary fence down to cross another ladder-stile. Turn RIGHT down the path past a pylon, through a small gate, to an access track of a nearby house. Do a sharp U-turn LEFT down a stony path to cross a stone bridge over the river to join the road beyond by Glan Hesgin and Efrog Newydd cottages. Return along your outward route to Canolfan Tryweryn, then follow the riverside path to the Centre (Sandy Buttle building), then roadside paths to the car park.

WALK 21
Y BALA TO LLANUWCHLLYN

DESCRIPTION A 7 mile scenic linear walk following the northern section of Snowdonia National Park's (SNP) waymarked upland trail around Llyn Tegid across the foothills, reaching a height of 918 feet/280 metres, and offering good views of Arenig and Arans mountains. Allow about 4½ hours. Refreshments in Llanuwchllyn at the Eagle Inn and Bala Lake Railway cafe in season.
START Loch Café [SH 921355].
DIRECTIONS Use roadside parking or SNP car park at the southern end of Llanuwchllyn, then take the T3 GHA bus from the bus stop by Station Road. Alight near the Leisure Centre in Y Bala and walk back to Loch Café, by the entrance to the lakeside car park. Another option is to combine the walk with a return scenic ride on Bala Lake Railway [www.bala-lake-railway.co.uk]..

I Go along the pavement above the tree-lined edge of the lake, past Fronfeuno SNP car park and the entrance to Mary Jones World. Just beyond the Llanycil road sign cross the road and go through the middle (Fron Feuno farm) of three entrances. Follow the waymarked bridleway up the stony track to a finger post on its bend. Go half-LEFT and follow the waymarked path up to a stile, then through a wood to another stile. Continue up the right-hand edge of a long reed/thistle covered field to a finger post at the top. Turn sharp LEFT angling away from the boundary down to a footbridge and up to a small gate. Go up the field to another small gate, and across the next field to a large gate and on between cottages. Cross Bala Caravan Park's driveway – *with 19thC Plas Moel y Garned nearby* – and continue ahead along a lane past a house and on to a stile.

2 Go across the undulating field to a stile, then the next to a ladder-stile near Moel-y-garnedd-uchaf farm. Go along a green track ahead to cross a sleeper bridge and ladder-stile. Go down the field edge to cross a ladder-stile near outbuildings. Join a nearby rising track, which soon bends right and

continues across a field to ladder-stile/gate. Go across the next field towards distant Ty'n-y-rhos cottage in trees and a ladder-stile just beyond. Follow a path across Gwastadros heathland beneath Moel y Garnedd past a finger post to cross a footbridge/stile at the corner of a small plantation. Walk round the edge of the plantation and along the field edge to a road. Follow it LEFT.

3 After ¹/₃ mile take the signposted SNP path over a stile on the right. Now follow the stiled waymarked path through several fields to Llwyn-mawr-uchaf farm. Pass to the left of conifers and buildings to a ladder-stile. Angle RIGHT to join a green track to cross a ladder-stile beyond the fence corner.
Go half-RIGHT to

follow telegraph poles down to a ladder-stile. Descend steeply to a ladder-stile below onto a track. Follow it LEFT round past Llwyn-mawr-isaf, then follow its driveway, later alongside the river, to the road. Turn LEFT, then at cottages follow the signposted SNP permissive path through a gate on the right and up Tyn Llechwedd's access track to a finger post, where the track splits.

4 Follow the right fork past sheepfolds and up through a waymarked gate. Continue along the track to gates at a cattle grid. On the bend, follow the signposted path ahead along the edge of Coed Swch

Gwastadros

caravan site

Y Bala

Loch Cafe ① bus stops

A494

Llanycil

Leisure Centre

halt

WALK 21

N

0 ¼ mile

A494

L l y n   T e g i d

B4403

Llangower

WALK 22

Bryncocyn

at the nonconformist chapel you will pass shortly, and founder of an Independent College in Y Bala. His son, Michael D Jones, who also lived here, succeeded his *father as Principal, and was a leading figure in the successful plan to establish a 'New Wales' in Patagonia, South America, with the first settlers leaving in 1865.* Continue to a waymarked gate then turn LEFT past a stone barn, and follow the waymarked gated path along the edge of two fields to a road. Follow it ahead, shortly passing the imposing chapel and its three storey house. Just beyond take the signposted path on the left and follow this chapel path to the A494. Cross the bridge with care, go past houses then cross the road and follow the pavement into Llanuwchllyn. *At the village entrance are the statues of two eminent local Welshmen. Sir Owen Morgan Edwards (1858–1920), regularly punished for speaking Welsh whilst at school, later became Chief Inspector of the new Welsh Education Department established in 1907. He actively promoted Welsh learning, writing many books and magazines. His son – Sir Ifan ab Owen Edwards (1895-1970) founded the Urdd Gobaith Cymru (The Welsh League of Youth) – which blends together culture, artistic activity, outdoor pursuits and Christian piety.* Continue through the village past the Eagles inn and church to eventually reach Station Road.

y Pentre woodland to cross a footbridge over a stream then a stile into a field. Continue ahead across the large field to go through a gate in the reedy left-hand corner. *Just to the south is the site of the Roman fort of Caer Gai built on an important strategic route and garrisoned from AD 75-130.* Turn RIGHT and follow the signposted path along the reedy field edge to a stile. Continue along the bottom of the next sloping field soon descending to cross a stile by the stream/forest. Continue down the edge of reedy terrain to cross a stile and footbridge over the stream on the right. Turn LEFT along the stony track to a lane by Erw Fron.

5 Turn RIGHT to the unassuming stone house of Weirglodd Wen – *the former home of Michael Jones, who was minister*

WALK 22

LLANUWCHLLYN TO Y BALA

DESCRIPTION A 7 mile scenic linear walk, apart from the beginning, following the southern section of Snowdonia National Park's waymarked upland trail around Llyn Tegid). The route meanders across the foothills on the south-east side of Llyn Tegid, reaching a height of 1083 feet/330 metres and enjoying extensive views of the lake throughout. The Bala Lake Railway (4 trains daily and café in season – www.bala-lake-railway.co.uk) also provides an opportunity to combine the walk with a scenic lakeside railway ride..

START Station Road, Llanuwchllyn [SH 878299].

DIRECTIONS Take the T3 GHA bus from Y Bala to Station Road at the southern end of Llanuwchllyn. If using the lakeside SNP car park by Loch cafe, the bus can be taken from near Stryd-y-Fron on the A494 beyond the entrance to the Leisure Centre. If starting from the town centre, there is a bus stop near Ye Olde Bulls Head on High Street, and a choice of return link paths from the lake at the end.

Take the no through road signposted to Bala Lake Railway to reach the station. Go through the car park, past the engine sheds and alongside the line. (This is a permissive section by kind agreement of the Railway. Do not walk along the track.) Shortly follow a waymarked path across the line and a small footbridge, then up the reedy field to the road. Follow it LEFT past Felindre, then take the signposted SNP path on the right up two fields, then an access track. At a finger post just below Llechweddystrad farm turn RIGHT up to a stile/gate and another nearby. Follow a permissive path behind outbuildings and down to a stony track. Turn RIGHT and follow the track up to its end at outbuildings (Ty'n y rhos). Cross a stile and go up the field to another. Go along the edge of two fields and past the end of Ffridd Gymen.

2 Go down the house's rough access track. Shortly, bend RIGHT with the track on the signposted SNP permissive path along a field edge to a gate. Follow the stony track

down to a stream and on through nearby Pantymarch farm. Continue along its access road. Later, at the end of woodland take the signposted SNP permissive path up a stony track on the right, then along a farm track to Bryncocyn. Go through the gated farmyard. Just beyond turn LEFT down to a stile/gate, then above a dingle to a finger post. Descend to a gate and footbridge and up into a field. Continue ahead to a stile, then go down to Ty Cerrig farm. Pass a barn to a gate and a stile below. Cross a footbridge and go through stiles/gates ahead. Go along the field edge to a further stile/gate, then descend a sunken tree-lined path to a stile to reach a stony track below. Follow it down to a concrete bridge over the river and up to a minor road. Follow it along the valley.

3 Shortly take the signposted SNP path up a track on the right past farm buildings and up towards Pant yr Onen. Follow the signposted SNP path behind the house and through a gate beyond. Follow the waymarked path alongside the fence up through a large then small gate. Follow the fence across the tree-covered hillside to a finger post. Descend a nearby stream guided by yellow topped posts. After about 120 yards cross it, then angle LEFT down to cross a stile, a footbridge over a stream, and stile beyond. Continue beside the fence, later

38

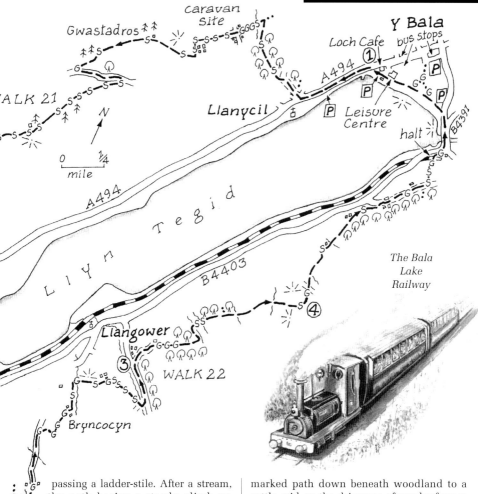

Gwastadros

caravan site

Y Bala

Loch Cafe   bus stops

A494   ①

ALK 21

N

Llanycil

Leisure Centre

halt

0   ¼
mile

A494

L l y n   T e g i d

B4403

The Bala Lake Railway

Llangower

WALK 22

③

Bryncocyn

②

passing a ladder-stile. After a stream, the path begins a steady climb up Brynau Goleu hillside to eventually cross a stile at a great viewpoint.

4 Just beyond turn LEFT down a green track to a minor road. Briefly go down the road, then follow the signposted SNP path down across the open hillside towards Y Bala, at a stream turning LEFT down across tussocky, then bracken covered ground to a stile. The path continues down beside a boundary to a cottage, then bends RIGHT up to a waymarked fence end. It now descends steadily beside the old fence, passes a wood corner and continues down a field past a house to a stile. Follow the way-

marked path down beneath woodland to a cattle grid on the driveway of nearby former Bala Lake Hotel – *now a holiday centre for John Lewis Partnership staff*. Pass behind the main building, through the rear car park and continue along a track past Rhos Fawr. Shortly, cross a stile on the left, and go down two fields, then across a footbridge over Bala Lake Railway and on to the B4403. Cross the old bridge opposite and go along the pavement beside the B4391, then side road past the end of the lake. At a car park, follow the signposted Tegid Way along a surfaced path near the shoreline of the lake, past two side paths leading to a car park and town centre, to eventually pass behind the Leisure Centre to reach the lakeside SNP car park.

PRONUNCIATION

These basic points should help non-Welsh speakers

Welsh	English equivalent
c	always hard, as in cat
ch	as in the Scottish word loch
dd	as th in then
f	as f in of
ff	as ff in off
g	always hard as in got
ll	no real equivalent. It is like 'th' in then, but with an 'L' sound added to it, giving 'thlan' for the pronunciation of the Welsh 'Llan'.

In Welsh the accent usually falls on the last-but-one syllable of a word.

KEY TO THE MAPS

- ➡ Walk route and direction
- ═ Metalled road
- ─ ─ ─ Unsurfaced road
- •••• Footpath/route adjoining walk route
- ∿ River/stream
- 🌲 Trees
- ▬ Railway
- **G** Gate
- **S** Stile
- **F.B.** Footbridge
- ☼ Viewpoint
- **P** Parking
- **T** Telephone
- Caravan site

THE COUNTRY CODE

- Be safe – plan ahead and follow any signs
- Leave gates and property as you find them
- Protect plants and animals, and take your litter home
- Keep dogs under close control
- Consider other people

Open Access

Some routes cross land where walkers have the legal right of access under the CRoW Act 2000. Access can be subject to restrictions and closure for land management or safety reasons for up to 28 days a year. Please respect any notices. Visit: www.naturalresources.wales for more information.

I wish to thank Gwynedd Council and Arwel Morris, the Snowdonia National Park Authority Llyn Tegid Warden. I remain indebted to Ifor Owen for sharing his wonderful knowledge of this area's history.

About the Author

David is an experienced walker with a love of the countryside and an interest in local history. He is the author of a series of walks guidebooks covering North Wales, where he has lived and worked for many years, as well as a freelance writer for Walking Wales magazine. He has worked as a Rights of Way surveyor across North Wales and served as a member of Denbighshire Local Access Forum.

Whether on a riverside ramble, mountain or long distance walk, he greatly appreciates the beauty, culture and history of the landscape and hopes that his comprehensive guidebooks will encourage people to explore on foot its diverse scenery and rich heritage. For more information visit www.davidberrywalks.co.uk

Published by **Kittiwake Books Limited**
3 Glantwymyn Village Workshops, Glantwymyn, Machynlleth, Montgomeryshire SY20 8LY
© Text & map research: David Berry 2016
www.davidberrywalks.co.uk
© Maps & illustrations: Kittiwake 2016.
First edition 2004. New edition 2008. Revised edition 2014. New edition 2016.
Illustrations by Morag Perrott
Cover photographs: *Main:* Cwm Glyn, Walks 11 & 12; *inset:* former town hall, Y Bala, Walk 1 David Berry
Care has been taken to be accurate. However neither the author nor the publisher can accept responsibility for any errors which may appear, or their consequences. If you are in doubt about any access, check before you proceed.
Printed by Mixam, UK.
ISBN: 978 1 908748 32 4